The Road Ahead . . .

Why Are We Driving
21st-Century Cars
on 20th-Century Roads
With 19th-Century Thinking?

Philip Tarnoff

Strategic Book Group

Strategic Book Group
P.O. Box 333
Durham CT 06422
www.StrategicBookClub.com

ISBN: 978-1-61204-532-0

Book Design: Suzanne Kelly

Acknowledgments

IT HAS BECOME A TRADITION OF THE PUBLISHING industry for authors to begin a book with the acknowledgment of support received from the various individuals and organizations during the preparation of their book. The practice is so ubiquitous that one sometimes wonders whether the lavish expressions of gratitude are sincere or merely a reflection of an ongoing tradition.

Please be assured that in the case of *The Road Ahead* (the book you are about to read), the acknowledgments are quite sincere. This book, which was written by a new author unsure of the value of his work, would not have seen the light of day without the assistance of the individuals I acknowledge.

First and most important, I would like to thank my loving and patient wife, Nancy, of nearly fifty years, for her support and encouragement. Without her, this book would not have been possible. In addition to spending many evenings without my companionship while I toiled on the manuscript, she was an invaluable critic of my writing and at the same time provided the needed encouragement to proceed. Her presence was essential to the unexpectedly monumental task of writing a factual, yet interesting, book on a subject that is less fascinating to the layperson than to the practitioners in the field.

Not far behind Nancy's significant contributions are those of Kevin Boras, editor of *Thinking Highways*. Kevin's contributions are too numerous to list but include the design of the cover, the posting of the book on the *Thinking Highways* website, editing the text, and extremely useful comments regarding its content. He also created the deadline pressure that is essential for turning a casual labor of love into a final product. In short, he moved the publication of the book from a vague thought to reality

Many authors and would-be authors are aware of the difficulties associated with writing the first chapter of a book—whether fiction or non-fiction. It is essential that the first chapter grab the readers so that they will want to continue reading the book. At the same time, the first chapter must set the stage for the rest of the book, providing the needed background for the material to be covered. Fiction writers have it easy. Their first chapters can begin with a major catastrophe, which might be a murder, a holocaust, a kidnapping, or some other event that rivets readers' interest while they try to anticipate the outcome of the introductory catastrophe. The writer of a factual text is faced with the daunting task of introducing a potentially dry subject in a manner that will entice the reader to continue reading. In this age when first chapters are given away by Google, Amazon, and Barnes and Noble to encourage the purchase of a book, the pressure on the author to create a powerful first chapter is further increased. I was no exception to the writer's block associated with the first chapter. My volunteer reviewers were brutally honest about my initial attempts at a first chapter that I had thought would be fascinating. They furnished me with comments such as, "The first chapter is boring, but I really enjoyed the second chapter which was very interesting." After no fewer than four attempts, a first chapter was created that won the acclaim of the volunteers, including my wife, Nancy; Kevin Boras; my son, David; my close friend and business associate John MacGowan; and my stereotypical National Public Radio (NPR) listeners Cynthia and Rupert Rossetti. So if the first chapter doesn't entice you to read the entire book, blame the reviewers. However, if you find the first chapter to be interesting and informative, they must receive the majority of the credit.

Without the assistance of the individuals acknowledged here, this book, which carries an important message for all U.S. citizens, would not have seen the light of day.

Table of Contents

FIGURES

Preface

SOME WOULD CALL TRANSPORTATION A NICHE MAR-
ket; others would call it a curious little business—invisible to
the general public. Whatever it's called, those responsible for
the nation's complex roadway system are overseeing a system
on which conditions are deteriorating at an alarming rate, with
little help in sight. Few appreciate the impact of this deterioration on the nation's economy, but its impact will become all
too obvious if the current rate of decay is allowed to continue.
The deterioration addressed here is not physical deterioration in
terms of potholes and bridge collapses, rather it is deterioration
in the way that the roadway infrastructure is operated.

When you sit at a traffic signal with no cars on the cross
street, when you see lanes closed for paving during heavy traffic, when you get caught in traffic due to accidents without any
warning, you are experiencing poor operations.

The tools for solving these problems are available but rarely
used to their full potential. So this is a story of unmet potential
and hope. It is a story that lays the groundwork for a discussion
of solutions that may be drastic. A reader with the patience to
absorb the information presented here will emerge with a better
understanding of the problem, and more importantly, with some
ideas of possible remedies.

The story begins in colonial days with the construction of the
nation's first highways. But for me, the story begins in January
1970 when I joined the Federal Highway Administration as an
eager young engineer, anxious to apply the latest technology to
the problems of traffic signal control. I had been intrigued with
this technology ever since reading a *Popular Science* magazine
article describing IBM's installation of computers for controlling traffic signals in San Jose, California and in Wichita Falls,
Texas. Having recently received a master's degree in electrical

engineering specializing in feedback control systems, it seemed to me that improvements in traffic signal control would be easy to accomplish. After all, how hard could it be? You measure the traffic flow, you adjust the times when the green is displayed, and you move the traffic. I've spent the remaining forty years answering the question, "How hard could it be?" The answers are complex and not at all obvious.

The public's impatience with those responsible for the management of our transportation system is understandable in an age of electronic marvels. If the technology exists to design and build robotic vacuum cleaners or unmanned aerial vehicles (UAVs), why do we have to wait at red lights when there is no traffic on the cross street? The public wonders when they can expect to purchase cars that guide themselves and operate on uncongested, safe roadways. Their frustration with the lack of progress is understandable given the daily announcements of exciting technological advances in so many other fields.

During the early 1990s, a much-heralded program was developed by the federal government to accelerate the use of electronics technology by the transportation community. This program is known as Intelligent Transportation Systems or ITS. Some feel that this name as an oxymoron, since today's systems are far from intelligent. The promise of ITS was a revolutionary change in the way that the transportation system is managed. ITS was (and still is) intended to span the entire range of transportation management functions, including traveler information, transit management, highway management (in both urban and rural areas), and commercial vehicle (truck) operations.

In its early days, many predicted that ITS would develop into the electronic equivalent of the current interstate system, since it was expected to revolutionize the way in which we travel. The promise of ITS included significant reductions in crashes, improved mobility, increased roadway capacity, reduced fuel consumption, improved air quality, increased personnel productivity, and enhanced corporate competitiveness.

Unfortunately, the results have been quite different. Since the original ITS strategic plan was prepared in 1992, highway fatalities have increased 9.6 percent, person hours of delay have increased 44 percent and fuel consumption has increased nearly 23 percent. With few exceptions, the domestic ITS industry has retained its focus on North America, and foreign competition in the United States has increased. As Dr. Joseph Sussman of MIT observed in his comments regarding the 1992 strategic plan, "There was clearly much the writing team and the ITS community . . . did not understand."[1]

How could the promise of ITS fail to materialize in an age of rapidly advancing technology, significant federal funding, and increasing transportation needs? What happened to cause an opportunity with so much potential to become the disappointment of an entire industry? While there is no single answer to this question, there is a unifying theme—that of a culture made up of politicians, policy makers, public agency employees, and manufacturers who are unprepared to aggressively exploit the promise of new technologies. Further complicating the picture is the fact that the transportation community primarily consists of two sectors: One sector is made up of those who specialize in the design and construction of civil works (highways, bridges, and rail systems). The other sector is one whose business is vehicle manufacturing (automobiles, buses, trains, etc.). Few in either sector understand the technology associated with ITS, and neither sector particularly enjoys dealing with the other.

The ITS initiative was developed by a group of individuals (including the author) with engineering backgrounds. Few members of this group appreciated the institutional hurdles to be overcome before information and electronics technology would be fully and routinely accepted as a critical element of the highway system. In short, to quote Pogo, "We have met the enemy, and they are us." The definition and plans for ITS were initially flawed, there was inadequate buy-in from the organizations responsible for its implementation, and there was an inadequate institutional structure to encourage its use. Perhaps most important, the public wasn't convinced of the potential of ITS and improved operations and remains unconvinced to this day of its ability to solve today's transportation problems. Absence of public support translates into the absence of political support, which in turn results in the absence of adequate funding.

Many have argued that the only way to ensure that the highway system is managed more efficiently and that transportation services are returned to acceptable levels of performance is through the creation of new organizations with the knowledge, incentive, and flexibility needed to take advantage of rapidly advancing technology. Major changes of this nature may be required before the promise of improved transportation system management is delivered.

But all is not lost. The technology exists to make a difference. What is missing is the political will to require (or at least encourage) its implementation. In a democracy, political will is frequently an outgrowth of public outcry. Have we lowered the bar of transportation system operations to such an extent that the public does not expect the operators of the system to provide better service? Or will the outcry eventually grow to the point where either today's system operations will improve or they are replaced by new institutions? Read on—the answers can be uncovered in the following chapters.

Nothing discussed here is intended as a criticism of the hard working staffs of public sector agencies. The majority of individuals working in the public sector are fully dedicated toward providing high quality transportation services for the traveling public. They labor under a myriad of archaic regulations and procedures, answer to elected officials with little or no understanding of the technical aspects of their jobs, and work within an environment of uncertain funding. In short, today's transportation agencies are asked to deal with monumental and growing problems in a Byzantine environment.

The intent of this book is to frame a debate about the missed opportunities of the past and the promise of the future. Perhaps most important, in Chapter 11, the book contains a novel and promising proposal for restructuring the transportation system in a manner that will ensure greater attention to operations, while at the same time removing the damaging political processes that determine investment priorities (sometimes with a healthy dose of pork). This is an important debate since the future of transportation in the United States, and indeed the health of the U.S. economy, depends on its conclusion. Two themes are presented in the following chapters. The first deals with the public-sector culture and its orientation to building new roads as opposed to operating them efficiently (i.e., nineteenth-century institutions). The second deals with the Byzantine environment. Combined, these themes add up to a twentieth-century highway system that is struggling to accommodate the needs of the twenty-first century. The book concludes with a number of positive suggestions for moving the system into the twenty-first century.

CHAPTER 1

A Colorful History—An Abridged Version

*Everywhere is within walking distance if you
have the time.*

—Steven Wright[2]

~~~~~~

The Age of Expeditions and Trails

In The Beginning

The sun glinting through the leaves of the forest canopy shone in the patient's face as he squinted through half-closed eyes from the bed of the jolting wagon. With the consuming illness that racked his body and the July heat of western Maryland, it was difficult to appreciate the beauty of the forest, but George was determined to ignore the discomfort of the malady that had consumed him shortly after departing from Fort Cumberland. He wanted to focus on the challenges of the upcoming confrontation with the French at a location that would eventually become the city of Pittsburgh.

The pace of the wagon would try the patience of a lesser man. Crawling along at a rate of five or six miles a day, the horses followed a twelve-foot-wide swath being cut through the forest by the 1,300 soldiers who made up the Braddock expedition. Using axes, shovels and other hand tools, the shirtless, sweating men were forced to carve a primitive road through the dense woods of western Maryland and Pennsylvania in their efforts to reach

1

the confluence of the Allegheny and Monongahela rivers where Fort Duquesne was being constructed by the French to claim this strategic location. The creation of this primitive passage (it could hardly be considered a road) was a monumental feat requiring an army for its successful completion.

However, the future father of the country was not reflecting upon the wonders of highway construction. He had contracted an illness with flu-like symptoms from which he suffered during most of the trip. The rough wagon ride and the heat made the trip even less bearable. Not a breeze was stirring as Lieutenant Colonel Washington lay on the hard bed of the wagon. He tried to analyze alternative strategies for confronting the French and their Indian allies in the battle that was to herald the start of the seven-year war, which became known as the French and Indian war. To Washington, it was obvious that the time-honored European battle traditions using neat formations with ranks of disciplined soldiers would have to be abandoned in favor of the colonial and Indian approach of sniping at each other from the cover of the forest. If only he could convince General Braddock of its wisdom, as he had previously convinced Braddock of the importance of splitting his three-thousand-man army into two units; the first, a more agile force of 1,300 soldiers which, with Washington, was proceeding to Fort Duquesne. This *flying column* included the scouts that led an advanced party of three hundred grenadiers and American militia units whose job was to protect the working party of three hundred men who were constructing the road. Construction was performed by cutting down trees and blasting the stumps using the same powder that was used for the cannons. Behind these activities was a one-mile procession that included the main force, artillery pieces, supply wagons, and at the end of this procession were the camp followers. Braddock himself rode near the front of the main force, decked out in a red uniform with gold trim, surrounded by his personal guards.

Neither Lieutenant Colonel George Washington nor the army that surrounded him realized that they were at the vanguard of two revolutions. The first, well known worldwide, was the revolution that led to the formation of the United States. The second, less well known and largely unrecognized, resulted from the efforts of the men hacking their way through the forest. This second revolution represented the first step in the creation of a mighty transportation system, without which the United States and other countries of the civilized world would never have reached their full potential. In retrospect, the second unknown revolution is likely to have had a greater and certainly more constructive impact on civilization than all the battles it was intended to support.

The significance of the construction of a path from Fort Cumberland to Pittsburgh was in no way diminished by the unfortunate conclusion of Braddock's attack on Fort Duquesne. General Braddock was a sixty-year-old career soldier with no combat experience. To make matters worse, he was unaware of the geography, politics, and people in the colonies and in the general vicinity of his expedition. He had been told by his superiors to expect fifteen miles of mountainous terrain, but instead he encountered more than fifty miles of steep slopes and impassible ridges. As a final nail in the coffin of the expedition, he managed to offend the potential Indian allies who could have provided assistance, with the result that they refused to accompany him.[3] Truly a comedy of errors and incompetence.

Ignoring Washington's advice, Braddock chose to organize his forces using English-style fighting techniques. On July 9, 1755, the British grenadiers saw the French and Indian fighters approaching through the trees of the forest. The British grenadiers made initial headway by firing volleys from their neatly formed ranks at the attacking force. However, their advantage evaporated as the inferior force of French and Indian fighters attacked the flanks of the British troops from the natural cover of the forest. When the fighting was over, 456 British soldiers had been killed and 422 were wounded.[4] Only 300, including Lieutenant Colonel Washington, escaped the catastrophe. Braddock was wounded and died on July 14 after having been carried away from the battlefield on a makeshift stretcher made from his own sash. He was buried in the middle of the newly constructed roadway, and the British troops marched over his grave in order to obliterate any signs of its presence so that the Indians would not desecrate the corpse.[5] Washington comported himself valiantly, receiving four bullet holes in his coat, and having two horses shot out from under him,[6] further enhancing his reputation as a soldier and leader.[7]

The crude path that had been constructed between Ft. Cumberland and Pittsburgh eventually became US Route 40, which was ultimately demoted to Alternate (Alt) US 40. The path followed by the Braddock expedition eventually became the route that was generally followed by Interstate 68, a beautiful scenic byway through the mountains of western Maryland. See Figure 1 that shows the three routes, including the parapet of the Casselman Bridge of the 1813 National Road, US Route 40, and I-68. Traveling on I-68, it is easy to overlook the significance of the Braddock expedition's accomplishments two and a half centuries earlier.

FIGURE 1   The Three Roads of Braddock's Trail

A Different Perspective

Forget the famous ride of Paul Revere warning the citizens of Boston that the "British are coming." His accomplishments are dwarfed by those of Israel Bissell, another American patriot who rode 345 miles from Watertown, Massachusetts to Philadelphia, Pennsylvania in the almost impossible time of four days and six hours beginning April 19, 1775. He rode to alert the American colonists living in the small towns along his route about the battle of Lexington, whose occurrence signaled the beginning of the Revolutionary War.[8] Bissell carried a message given to him by Colonel Joseph Palmer of Braintree in the Colony of Massachusetts, which said in part:

> The bearer Israel Bissell is charged to alarm the country quite to Connecticut, and all persons are desired to furnish him with fresh horses, as they may be needed. I have spoken with several who have seen the dead and wounded at Lexington and Concord.[9]

Bissell's travels were facilitated by the Boston Post Road (now known as US Route 1) which had ironically been established by King Charles II of England in 1673 to carry the mail from lower Manhattan, in New York City, to Boston.

While there have been many attempts to separate the facts from the fiction of Bissell's ride (including his name, which some claim was Isaac Bissell, and whether the ride was made by one person—Bissell—or included multiple riders), the indisputable aspect of his accomplishment is that it was enabled by a road whose existence began, like many of the U.S. highways, as an Indian trail. This trail was so heavily used by many generations of the Algonquin Indians that it became a path worn several feet deep by the time of the British arrival in New England. Although its first English name was the Pequot Path, it was subsequently renamed the Boston Post Road because of its primary function of facilitating the movement of mail among the villages it connected. The first post rider on the continent rode along the Post Road, traveling through New Haven, Hartford, Brookfield, Worcester, and Cambridge, cities that became known as terminal cities along the road.

During his tenure as postmaster general, Benjamin Franklin had stone mile markers installed along the roadway. The mile markers served as the basis for calculation of postage, which was based on the distance that the mail was carried. Some of these mile markers remain in existence to this day.

The Post Road was the beginning of US Route 1 that became the major north-south artery of the East Coast, covering nearly 2,400 miles from Fort Kent, Maine to Key West, Florida. US 1 meanders through numerous towns and cities, such that modern long distance travel using Route 1 would be a trial to any but the most patient traveler. The route traverses such historic areas as Harvard Square in Cambridge, Massachusetts and Wall Street in New York City. By some estimates, there is an average of one Dunkin Donuts shop every two miles along the road.[10]

US 1 was ultimately displaced by Interstate 95 (I-95) as a transportation facility for the long distance traveler. Although I-95 is frequently congested, it would be difficult to imagine the level of congestion that would exist on US 1 if it were to carry the same levels of traffic.

Taming of the West

The East Coast does not have a monopoly on roads with historic beginnings. Many other U.S. highways have colorful backgrounds. One example is the El Camino Real (Spanish for the Royal Road), known as the California Mission Trail. This six-hundred-mile (966-km) route connects the Mission San Francisco Solano in Sonoma in the north with the Mission San Diego do Alcala to the south. The trail was established by the Spanish to support commerce in the California territory, with missions (outposts) located at approximate intervals of thirty miles (48-km), the equivalent of a long one-day horseback ride. Its existence began with the construction of the San Diego mission in 1769, not long before the onset of the Revolutionary War. The final northernmost mission in San Francisco was completed in 1823. The legend of the trail is that monks spread mustard seed along its route to mark its location by the plant's yellow flowers.[11]

The El Camino Real was initially used, as were its East Coast counterparts, to support the movement of people, goods, and mail along the western coast. The trail evolved into today's modern highways in a similar manner to that of US 40 in Western Maryland and US 1 along the East Coast. Major sections of the El Camino Real became US 101 and ultimately Interstate 5.

No history of the evolution of trails into highways would be complete without mentioning the Oregon Trail and the Santa Fe Trail. The former served as the primary route for settlers traveling from Independence, Missouri to Oregon and other points in the newly opened west. The trail became a major route to the west in 1843 due to a surge of settlers hoping for a better life than the one they had in the East and Midwest during the depression of the late 1830s. This grueling two-thousand-mile trail roughly paralleled US Route 30 and ultimately Interstate 84.

The Santa Fe Trail was used primarily by fur traders traveling from Independence, Missouri to Santa Fe, New Mexico. This trail followed a more southerly route than the Oregon Trail. The trail was heavily used during the 1850s for the movement of soldiers and supplies to support the United States in its war with Mexico. The trip from Independence to Santa Fe took approximately eight weeks. Although the trail fell into disuse with the completion of the Santa Fe railroad in 1880, portions of I-25 currently follow its route.

The common denominator of these trails as well as their numerous less well-known counterparts was their important role in the development of the western United States. They supported the movement of freight, farm produce and animals, postal service, and wartime goods, and served as essential facilities for the movement of settlers throughout the Midwest and West. Their evolution from Indian trails to critical transportation facilities demonstrated the important role they played in the development of the United States.

The Age of the Turnpike

Wagons and Stagecoaches

The Conestoga wagon, developed in the Conestoga Valley of Lancaster County, Pennsylvania, was used to carry people, household goods, merchandise, and farm produce from the factories and farms of the east to the new frontier. First introduced around 1717, these conveyances became pervasive well before the end of the century. Carrying loads of up to eight tons and hauled by teams of oxen, mules, or horses, the Conestoga wagon was the equivalent of today's over-the-road tractor-trailers.

The stagecoach was the high-speed counterpart of the Conestoga wagon. Stagecoaches transported small numbers of people at a faster pace than could be provided by the plodding teams pulling the heavily loaded wagons that covered only approximately fifteen miles per day. The history of the stagecoach is quite different from that of the Conestoga wagon. First developed in England in the 1500s, it was in widespread use throughout Europe prior to its introduction in the United States. By the mid-1700s, stagecoach lines had proliferated in Boston and New York as an efficient form of transportation for both passengers and mail. While the routes in the East were relatively civilized, stagecoach transportation in the West was significantly more primitive, as described by the following excerpt taken from Wikipedia:[12]

> Coaches on the overland stages traveled continuously for twenty-two days, day and night, through dust or blowing sand, in intense heat or cold, sometimes tormented by insects, with only brief stops at way stations to change teams; passengers often had poor food and no rest. If a passenger got off the stage to rest, he might be stuck in that place for a week or more, or longer if the next stage had no available seats. Passengers were sometimes compelled to walk to relieve the fatigued teams or when the coach had to be lightened to make it over a stretch of sand or to help push coaches uphill or extricate them when bogged down in mud or sand.[13]

"Passengers crowded into coaches caused conditions that prompted Wells Fargo to post these rules in each coach for passenger behavior," examples of which include:

- If ladies are present, gentlemen are urged to forego smoking cigars and pipes as the odor of same is repugnant to the gentler sex. Chewing tobacco is permitted, but spit with the wind, not against it.

- Buffalo robes are provided for your comfort in cold weather. Hogging robes will not be tolerated and the offender will be made to ride with the driver.
- Don't snore loudly while sleeping or use your fellow passenger's shoulder for a pillow; he or she may not understand and friction may result.
- Firearms may be kept on your person for use in emergencies. Do not fire them for pleasure or shoot at wild animals as the sound riles the horses.
- In the event of runaway horses remain calm. Leaping from the coach in panic will leave you injured, at the mercy of the elements, hostile Indians, and hungry coyotes.
- Gents guilty of unchivalrous behavior toward lady passengers will be put off the stage. It's a long walk back. A word to the wise is sufficient.[14]

The speed of the stagecoach can be inferred from the U.S. Government's requirements for a $600,000 grant for mail service along the Butterfield Overland route from St. Louis, Missouri to San Francisco, California. To qualify for the grant, the mail had to be transported a distance of 2,812 miles within twenty-five days—an average distance of 112 miles per day through rugged terrain, hostile Indian tribes, uncertain weather, and numerous river crossings. Certainly a different pace than that of the Conestoga wagon.

Turnpikes

Imagine the excitement when the citizens of a local community learn that a private turnpike company was planning to build a road for easy travel between neighboring communities. The excitement escalates when they learn that the construction will occur at no cost to the taxpayers. In their enthusiasm to support these private enterprises, many citizens purchase shares in the turnpike companies without concern for receiving any significant return on their investment.

The construction of turnpikes and the accompanying emergence of the turnpike companies was a direct result of the introduction of stagecoaches and Conestoga wagons as modes of travel during the late 1700s. These conveyances needed improved roads that were passable during all seasons and weather conditions. Because the individual state governments could not afford the construction of high-quality facilities, they chartered turnpike companies operated and financed by private citizens; the Philadelphia and Lancaster Turnpike Road completed in 1795 is one such example. This privately financed sixty-two mile facility was constructed at a cost of $465,000. (At $7,500 per mile, this was quite a bargain compared to today's highway construction costs that currently approach $100 million per mile). Turnpikes soon became the predominant form of inter-urban roadway construction. These roads were constructed along the Indian and pioneer trails that had served foot and horse traffic prior to the introduction of wheeled transportation.

To this day, liberals and conservatives debate the appropriate rolls of the private and public sector as it relates to the construction and operation of critical infrastructure—particularly roadways. Nowhere have the relative merits of the two approaches been more apparent than in the private sector's emergence as significant owners and operators of the turnpikes. A stark comparison of the performance of the two sectors can be found in the comparison of two roads: the National Road built by the federal government, and the Pittsburgh Pike built by a consortium of five private companies. The sections of the two roads crossing the Appalachian Mountains roughly paralleled each other, and both were constructed in similar terrain. The National Road provided travel between Cumberland, Maryland and Wheeling, West Virginia, while the Pittsburgh Pike provided travel between Harrisburg and Pittsburgh, Pennsylvania. The federal government spent $13,455 per mile to complete the first two hundred miles of the National Road while the private sector consortium spent $4,805 per mile for the construction of the Pittsburgh Pike. In addition, the National Road rapidly deteriorated due to the uncertain government funding for maintenance while the Pittsburgh Pike remained in good repair due to the reliable funding stream generated by the tolls that were collected.[15] This stark comparison of construction costs and ongoing quality of service suggests that private sector ownership of infrastructure is far superior to that of the public sector.

Given the success of the Pittsburgh Pike, it is curious that privately operated turnpikes virtually disappeared by the beginning of the twentieth century. Their disappearance was due to the confluence of a number of factors including:

- The use of plank road construction used by the private sector for their turnpikes provided high quality transportation for four to five years, instead of the twelve years that had been predicted. At the end of its life, it rapidly deteriorated, and replacement was expensive.[16]
- The emergence of alternative forms of intercity transportation including canals and railroads competed with the turnpikes that relied on toll revenue for their continued existence.
- Public agencies increased their regulation of the turnpike companies, controlling the pricing and location of tolls without concern for the financial viability of these companies.
- There was a relatively low rate of financial return to investors.

When an important road is abandoned by its private sector owners, the public sector may often be required to assume ownership of the abandoned facility or construct a comparable facility to replace the transportation capabilities on which its constituency has come to depend. And therein lays the disadvantage of private sector ownership of civil infrastructure: the possibility that the private sector will abandon the enterprise if it does not generate an adequate profit, leaving the public sector with the responsibility for its continued operation. Thus, the relative merits of the two approaches (private versus public sector ownership) remain unresolved. Each approach offers different benefits, leading to polarization of a critical debate that is reemerging in the twenty-first century. These issues are discussed in greater detail in a later chapter.

The Age of the Highway

In a glorious confluence of events, the Duryea brothers, two bicycle mechanics from Springfield, Massachusetts, developed the first gasoline-powered conveyance. Known as a motor wagon, this device did not even include brakes but was stopped by driving it into a convenient curb or other obstacle. This development occurred in 1893 and was rapidly followed by the Wright Brothers' (two other bicycle mechanics) demonstration of powered flight in 1903 and Henry Ford's introduction of the Model T Ford in 1908.

While it is doubtful that the airplane had much of an impact on the development of America's highway system, bicycles and motorized transport had a tremendous affect. These rubber-tired vehicles required a smooth surface if they were to meet their full potential.

The development of the modern highway system began explosively during the Roaring Twenties with the creation of the Federal Bureau of Public Roads (BPR) whose responsibility it was to distribute the federal funding to the states for the development of a paved two-lane highway system. During the 1930s, the BPR supported the road building projects created by state and local governments to spur local employment and encourage the recovery of the local economy from the great depression. This same approach was utilized by the Obama administration in its stimulus spending of 2010 that was intended to accelerate recovery from the great recession of the twenty-first century. The burst of road building that occurred during the first half of the twentieth century was responsible for much of the thousands of miles of paved highways and local roads that make up today's transportation system.

The Age of the Interstate

Following the conclusion of the First World War, Secretary of War Newton D. Baker organized a transcontinental convoy whose purpose was "to service-test the special-purpose vehicles developed for use in the World War I, not all of which were available in time for such use, and to determine by actual experience the possibility and the problems involved in moving an army across the continent, assuming that railroad facilities, bridges, tunnels, and so on had been damaged or destroyed by agents of an Asiatic enemy."[17] The First Transcontinental Motor Convoy (FTMC) traveled from Washington, DC to San Francisco, California, departing on July 7, 1919. Lieutenant Colonel Dwight David Eisenhower was assigned to travel as an observer.

Even as early as 1919, the war department (today's department of defense) believed in doing things in a big way. The convoy included sixty-five vehicles, nine motorcycles, and nearly three hundred men. To say the least, the results of the trip were disappointing if not catastrophic. It took the convoy two months to complete the 3,200-mile trip, averaging slightly more than six miles per hour. During the trip, the War Department lost nine vehicles and twenty-one men. It was involved in 230 accidents during which the road failed due to vehicles sinking in quicksand or mud, running off the road, running over embankments, and so on. It also inadvertently destroyed eighty-eight bridges and culverts. If it hadn't been so sad, this trip could have been considered a comedy.

In the report that described the debacle, Lieutenant Colonel Eisenhower observed that "in many places excellent roads were installed some years ago that have since received no attention whatsoever. Absence of any effort at maintenance has resulted in roads of such rough nature as to be very difficult of negotiating."[18] Eisenhower was profoundly influenced by this experience. He learned that most of the nation's roadways were in horrible condition and incapable of supporting the needs of its military. These shortcomings were to be demonstrated even more dramatically during the Second World War of the 1940s.

During the Second World War, funding was made available to support the construction and maintenance of roads needed by the nation's military establishment for the movement of personnel and materiel. These roads connected major population centers, manufacturing facilities, and coastal ports. At the conclusion of this "war to end all wars," the nation's economy had recovered, but the federal budget had not. As a result of the fiscal shortages of the late 1940s, the highway system fell into disrepair, and congestion clogged the streets of the nation's cities. It appeared that the wonderful transportation system that had supported the war effort was in the process of disintegration and along with it, the vibrancy of the nation's economy.

At least in part due to his experience with the FTMC, President Eisenhower supported the fight for legislation authorizing the largest public works project in the history of the world. The legislation, which was passed on June 29, 1956, was considered by many to be the crowning achievement of his administration. The interstate system (also known as the National Defense Highway System as a result of the conclusions of the FTMC) offered and delivered on the promise of serving as the engine that drove the U.S. economy to its leadership role during the twentieth century.

To fans of statistics, the numbers are staggering. The system cost nearly $130 billion to construct.[19] It includes more than 46,000 miles of pavement, which by 2006 carried people on more than one trillion (that's 1,000,000,000,000) trips per year. The project required most of the fifty years since its beginning for its completion. Three-hundred-million cubic yards of concrete were used in its construction. If all of the steel reinforcing rods used in the system were placed end to end, they would reach the moon and back eleven times.[20]

Most Americans believe that the interstate system is owned and operated by the federal government. The public is generally unaware of the fact that, with the exception of some roadways for which the U.S. Park Service is responsible, all U.S. roadways are owned and operated by states, counties, or cities. In fact, the interstate system's design and construction standards were not even developed by the federal government but rather by the American Association of State Highway and Transportation Officials (AASHTO),[21] a little-known organization whose membership primarily consists of the state departments of transportation (DOTs). This powerful organization has a significant influence on the processes and standards that control the interstate system and most other state roads.

On Thursday, June 29, 2006, the nation celebrated the fiftieth birthday of the interstate system. Most people missed the big birthday bash! Even though they were invited, the majority of the U.S. population was not even aware of it. However, during the fifty years of its existence, the system had a significant impact on the American way of life. It reduced fatalities per million miles of travel by a factor of five, without question saving thousands of lives. It reduced the transcontinental travel time from months to days. It also reshaped our entire economy, culture, and demographics. This was unquestionably a crowning achievement—but was it?

While offering major improvements in safety and mobility to the American public, the system also encouraged major increases in long distance travel with its associated impact on gas consumption and pollution. It led to urban sprawl in regions such as Los Angeles, effectively destroying the concept of a central city with all of the advantages of focused development. It encouraged the existence of the two-car family—good for the auto industry, bad for congestion. It impaired our ability to develop transit systems that could serve employment, shopping, and entertainment centers, since these activity centers ceased to exist. It encouraged freight shipment by truck rather than rail, thus discouraging the development of a robust rail system in spite of the latter's superior energy efficiency. And an often-overlooked *fly in the ointment* was that the largest construction project in the world has led to the largest ongoing roadway maintenance and rehabilitation program in the world, a program that the nation can scarcely afford. In short, the interstate system has been a mixed blessing.

The Age of the Electronic Interstate

So the 1700s were the age of the trail, the 1800s were the age of the turnpike, and the 1900s were the age of the paved road and interstates. Give or take a few decades, each of these phases of development occurred within a hundred-year timeframe. Each step of the progression provided the foundation for the evolution of a nation that was increasingly vibrant and productive. To a certain extent, each of these phases also involved war or some sort of armed confrontation. During this evolution, the nation experimented with various forms of pavement, private ownership, and accommodation of differing forms of transportation. U.S. citizens can be justifiably proud of these are accomplishments.

But now what? What will the next phase of transportation look like? The interstate system is essentially complete, and all available highway funding is being used for the maintenance and rehabilitation of existing roads. Yet travel demand is continuing to increase without any apparent steps being taken at any level of government to take the nation's transportation system to the next level of performance and capacity.

Some have predicted that accelerating developments within the electronics and computer community offer the potential for the era of the electronic interstate system. There is some justification for this. For example, estimates have been made that an automated highway on which vehicles control their operation without human intervention could double the capacity of the existing interstate roadways. Other types of electronics offer the potential for reducing crash rates by more than 50 percent and travel delays by nearly 40 percent (more about this later). But does the country have the resources and the determination to take advantage of these capabilities? Or alternatively, will the governing bodies of the nation be willing to turn responsibility of the transportation system over to the private sector? Another alternative, albeit an unpleasant one, is to tolerate the gradual deterioration of a system on which hundreds of billions (perhaps trillions) of dollars have been spent and with it the deterioration of the nation's economy. These are important questions since their answer will determine our future quality of life.

Part I
The State of the Twentieth-Century System

It's congested and full of potholes, but how did it get that way?

CHAPTER 2

Highways To Heaven ... Or Is It Hell?

Congestion is not a fact of life. We need a new approach and we need it now.
—Norman Y. Mineta[22]

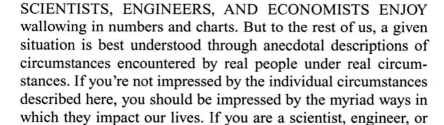

SCIENTISTS, ENGINEERS, AND ECONOMISTS ENJOY wallowing in numbers and charts. But to the rest of us, a given situation is best understood through anecdotal descriptions of circumstances encountered by real people under real circumstances. If you're not impressed by the individual circumstances described here, you should be impressed by the myriad ways in which they impact our lives. If you are a scientist, engineer, or economist, you will have to wait for Chapter 3, which quantifies the underlying causes of the problems illustrated by the anecdotes provided in this chapter. In the mean time, we begin by putting a *face* on the current state of the transportation system.

If these two chapters are successful, you should be convinced that we are on the verge of a transportation crisis that will require heroic measures if we are to prevent the further deterioration of the system in order to ensure the long-term health of the U.S. economy.

The Face of the Commuter

The BBC reported that a study of 125 commuters conducted in 2004 concluded that in many situations, commuters experi-

19

ence higher heart rates and blood pressures than those of combat fighter pilots or riot police. The five-year study also identified a mental condition labeled commuter amnesia during which the commuters forget large parts of their trip to work due to the stress they experience. The difference between commuters and either fighter pilots or police is that commuters feel as if they are in a situation they cannot control. Since the average commute included in the study was forty-five minutes, it concluded that people are turned into zombies for ninety minutes each day while undergoing extremely high levels of stress.[23] What a way to live.

Imagine the stress level associated with sudden congestion on an interstate roadway due to a truck crash (as I recently experienced) while commuting to an important meeting. My stress level was further increased when attempting to use an alternate route (a signalized arterial roadway). I ended up in worse congestion than the route that I had abandoned. My stress peaked as I crept along the arterial roadway, and at each intersection the traffic signals were stopping the heavy traffic that had diverted on the arterial along with me, while the side streets had very light traffic. A trip that should have taken an hour ended up as a three-hour commute, a commute with high blood pressure caused by the frustration of being stuck in traffic without reliable information about alternate routes. The frustration was compounded by the knowledge that the agency responsible for the traffic signal operation had failed to make any adjustments to accommodate the sudden surge in diverted traffic. This was a convincing demonstration by the transportation agency of its lack of concern for the public it served.

But my delays were caused by an incident. This condition is known as non-recurring congestion. How about the commuter doomed to sit patiently (or not so patiently) in endless daily (recurring) congestion?

In case you don't think that miserable commutes due to recurring congestion hurt the economy, consider the experience of a Northern Virginia business. According to their human relations (HR) director, a newly hired employee quit by cell phone on the first day of work after being stuck in traffic for two hours.

Think of the lost productivity of those who do not quit but sit in their cars for one to three hours a day. Remember that one hour of commuting represents the equivalent of two and a half working days of unproductive time each month, which translates into more than a month of unproductive time each year, time that, if not spent at work, could at least be spent with the family or on recreational activities. This pattern is repeating itself nationally and can be directly attributed to a loss of national productivity.

The Face of the Soccer Mom

As used here, the term *soccer mom* is intended to reflect male or female parents transporting their offspring and friends to extra-curricular activities, shopping, and social events—in short, any non-work activity. The distinguishing characteristic of this type of travel is that it typically occurs at times other than the commuting period and is not directional. In other words, while commuters travel from residential areas to employment centers, soccer moms travel in various unpredictable directions and do not adhere to a strict daily schedule.

The travel demands of the soccer mom are important because they illustrate some important, yet poorly appreciated, facts. First, mass transit (buses, commuter rail, etc.), which is generally viewed as the solution to all problems of urban congestion, energy consumption (aka oil imports), and emissions (air pollution), will not reduce congestion and other transportation problems caused by soccer moms. Because traffic patterns are not directional and are unpredictable, these solutions will not work. Could you picture a mother (or father) taking their offspring to a soccer game by bus? I've never seen it although my daughter was a champion soccer goalkeeper, and I've attended innumerable soccer practices and games. Second, because of its lack of directionality, soccer-mom traffic (aka off-peak traffic) is the most difficult to control. Signal timing is much more readily developed for conditions in which all traffic is flowing in the same direction. Random and unpredictable traffic flows are difficult to control. So the rapidly increasing traffic flow created by the soccer moms of the twenty-first century is difficult to manage. Even though off-peak traffic is lighter, the soccer moms require the same level of attention that the commuters receive.

Near Johnson City, Tennessee (east Tennessee to those of you who are geographically challenged), my son and daughter-in-law must not be late picking up their son from daycare or they will be charged a late fee of $1.00 per minute. They rely on the reliability of the transportation system to take them from their work at the local university to the daycare provider. While the Johnson City area is rural by East Coast standards, travel times can be unpredictable due to traffic incidents or inclement weather. Yes, they get ice storms and snow in Tennessee. Their situation is not unique. Many who have similar daycare issues have indicated that they would be willing to pay a road user fee if it meant a timely arrival at daycare. So road user fees are not only for the rich. The pejorative term Lexus Lanes that is frequently applied to the toll lanes that provide preferential service is misleading at best.

The Face of the Online Purchaser

The economy may be floundering, but you wouldn't know it if you were selling online. In 2009 e-commerce (the popular term for online shopping) sales were $32.4 billion, capturing an increasing percentage of total retail spending (a share of 3.6 percent in 2009 as opposed to the 3.3 percent share in 2008).[24] So while it is well known that we are increasingly using the Internet for shopping, it is less well known that this change in our purchasing habits has led to an equivalent change in the pressures on the transportation system.

The purchasing habits of e-commerce shoppers follow a predictable pattern beginning with purchases from known retailers (Target, Sears, Crate and Barrel, Talbots, Barnes & Noble, etc.) and eventual migration toward sellers specializing in online sales such as Amazon, eBay, and their lesser known counterparts. Anything can be purchased online, including groceries, drugs, repair parts, clothing . . . and of course, books. The convenience of e-commerce is impressive in that it eliminates the need to visit (or call) multiple retailers to find a desired product, as occurred while writing this chapter, when my wife wanted to locate fasteners for ironing board covers. Does anyone use these anymore? A five-minute search located the desired products, which were available from multiple sources.

So what does this have to do with transportation? It is significant in that the shopping trips to the mall or grocery store made by the individual are replaced by the delivery trucks of UPS and FedEx. This is a potentially more efficient system to say the least in that one truck can replace the trips of multiple single passenger automobiles cruising from one mall to the next. So the individual discretionary off-peak shopping trips are being displaced by the more efficient small package deliveries of e-commerce purchases—good news for the hard working traffic engineer but bad news for veteran shoppers.

Unfortunately, the positive effects of e-commerce are offset by increased travel associated with a wide variety of discretionary activities. In other words, shopping is in many cases a discretionary activity. To many, it is a form of entertainment. As a result, increased shopping efficiencies free up discretionary time for other activities, including visits to friends, sightseeing, travel, and so on. As a result, e-commerce is likely to have the negative impact of increasing the number of delivery trucks on the road without reducing the amount of discretionary shopping travel that takes place. While it is too early to be certain, so far, there is no evidence that off-peak travel is decreasing as a result of e-commerce or any other force, except possibly the short-lived impacts of increasing fuel prices.

The Face of the Shipper

Perhaps the dollars and cents costs of congestion can be quantified by trucking companies more than any other user of the system. During the 1980s, a representative of Federal Express (FedEx) told me that a reduction in average delivery times nationally by one minute would save the company more than one million dollars a day. Undoubtedly, the potential savings have increased significantly during the past thirty years. Imagine the negative impact of increased average delivery times by five or ten minutes on the costs of FedEx, United Parcel Service (UPS), and the United States Postal Service (USPS), not to mention the thousands of independent services throughout the United States. These costs are incalculable and result in an increase in shipping costs and charges. These increased costs will ultimately have a significant drag on the economy.

Freight is also shipped within the manufacturing system to transfer raw materials and partially fabricated parts between various manufacturers as part of the overall production cycle. This process is invisible to the average consumer but has as much of an impact on our economy as any other aspect of the trucking system. Manufacturers have found that they can save money by reducing their inventory of raw materials and partially completed parts using a process known as just-in-time (JIT) delivery. When JIT-delivery is used, manufacturers and/or retailers depend on their suppliers to ship enough parts and/or final products to ensure that the assembly line can continue without interruption and that store shelves are adequately stocked. The supplier, in turn, depends on the shipper to ensure that delivery times are met. JIT-delivery ensures the efficiency of the manufacturing and retail processes. It is an outstanding example of the impact of the transportation system on global competitiveness and economic health.

Not many realize that much of the credit for Toyota's success as an automobile manufacturer can be attributed to Henry Ford. His book *Today and Tomorrow* was required reading for all Toyota executives. In his book, the concept of *lean manufacturing* is applied to the automobile industry, a concept ignored by the American industry and revered by the Japanese. JIT-delivery is at the heart of the lean manufacturing concept, which is intended to minimize manufacturing inventories. If you don't believe that, consider the fact that during the 1980s, U.S. manufacturers were carrying $775 in parts inventory for every vehicle manufactured while the Japanese were carrying $150 of parts inventory for every vehicle manufactured.[25] This is a staggering difference considering that General Motors U.S. sold 3.5 million vehicles annually during the 1980s, with a resultant investment of more than $2 billion in excess inventory. Eventually, the U.S.

automakers changed their ways using JIT-delivery. As a result, the automobile industry, like most other U.S. manufacturers, became captives of the efficiency of the transportation system. Companies unable to depend on reliable transportation of raw materials and parts to their manufacturing facilities relocated overseas.

The downside of JIT-delivery is that it has increased the number of trucks on the road. For example, a truck delivering pizzas to a retail outlet cannot wait for a full load before leaving the loading dock. It must leave with a partial load if the pizzas are to arrive on time. The other equally significant downside of JIT-delivery is that it places increased responsibility on transportation agencies and the governmental agencies that fund them to create and manage a system that is efficient and reliable. The freight community and the enterprises it serves cannot afford the gradual deterioration of a system on which they have come to rely, but the deterioration is already underway.

The Face of the Government

In an article describing the impact of urban congestion on the prosperity of cities, *USA Today* described the situation in the following terms, "It seemed peculiar when the Chamber of Commerce, known for its unrestrained boosterism, called traffic congestion the greatest threat to Atlanta's continued economic prosperity. Cities now view bad traffic as much more than just a nuisance for harried commuters. It's bad public relations in the never-ending competition against other cities over the quality of life. Cities believe that out-of-control traffic congestion hurts their ability to attract new businesses. And in some places, gridlock is the political issue of the day"[26]

So traffic congestion is becoming a grass roots issue. As so often happens with grass roots issues, the federal government has captured it and rushed to take the lead in addressing its resolution.

The federal government's adoption of the issue of traffic congestion can be found in the statements of its leaders. In her testimony before the House Transportation and Infrastructure's Subcommittee on Highways and Transit, Federal Highway Administrator Mary E. Peters (who subsequently became the U.S. Secretary of Transportation) said, "Increased traffic congestion is a growing threat to the nation's economy and quality of life of all Americans." Peters delivered her testimony on May 21, 2002 during a subcommittee hearing on Relieving Highway Congestion through Capacity Enhancements and Increased Efficiency.

Peters asked for better coordination among the agencies involved with roadway operations, including traffic, public safety, parking, media, and first responders. She added that the environment, safety, and security of the highway system would be enhanced with expanded capacity, more efficient operations, and system preservation.[27]

It would be a simple matter to fill a book with hand-wringing statements about the state of America's surface transportation system. While the coordination among agencies being called for by Ms. Peters will definitely help, it is doubtful that increasing the discussions among sister agencies will make a noticeable difference. It is clear that much more fundamental improvements are needed that include both financing and organizational changes for the roadways of the present to become highways that serve the needs of the twenty-first century. This is not an abstract desire but a necessity if the United States is to maintain its economic leadership.

A Glimpse of the Future

The future of the U.S. transportation system will be discussed in the second section of this book. But after reading the preceding discussion of the existing system, one has to wonder where this is all going. *New Yorker* magazine recently published an article describing the roadway system in Moscow that begins with the statement that "Moscow's terrible traffic has been infamous for a while now, but in the past year it has come to feel like an existential threat."[28] The article describes nightmare situations of a city paralyzed by snowfalls in which an ambulance driver was standing beside his vehicle throwing snowballs lazily off an embankment. He'd been trapped in traffic so long that his patient was now dead. The article describes politicians whose black Mercedes are equipped with sirens so that they can travel in emergency lanes and ignore the traffic signals. It concludes with a road-rage story of a fight between a bicycle rider and the son of a politician who was driving a Lexus, which concluded with the bicycle rider smashing all the windows of the Lexus with a baseball bat. Will U.S. urban areas be experiencing these conditions? Possibly . . .

In his short story *The Queue*,[29] Vladimir Sorokin writes of the dialog among a long, slow-moving line of Russians waiting to purchase unspecified merchandise. The dialog alternates between idle chatter and anger at those who are entering the line ahead of them. Gradually, they become resigned to living in the queue, leaving the line frequently to take care of other errands. This story as a model of the transportation system is not as fanciful as it might appear. As we spend an increasingly high percentage of our lives sitting in traffic queues, we are beginning to adapt to the concept of living in our cars. With the increasing sophistication of in-vehicle electronics that provide telephone and Internet connections as well as various forms of entertainment, our cars have become a home away from home. Is this the depressing vision of the future? Are we doomed to spend our futures in our cars?

CHAPTER 3

The State of the System—Statistics Don't Lie

*Thanks to the Interstate Highway System, it is
now possible to travel across the country from
coast to coast without seeing anything.*
                                    —Charles Kuralt[30]

~~~~~~

THE TEXAS TRANSPORTATION INSTITUTE (TTI), AN
organization housed within Texas A&M University that pub-
lishes a well-known annual report that encapsulates the state
of the U.S. highway transportation system, quantified concerns
about the state of the U.S. highway system. In its most recent
report, published in 2009, the TTI researchers concluded that:

- The overall cost (based on wasted fuel and lost
  productivity) reached $87.2 billion in 2007—more than
  $750 for every U.S. traveler.
- The total amount of wasted fuel topped 2.8 billion
  gallons—three weeks' worth of gas for every traveler.
- The amount of wasted time totaled 4.2 billion hours—
  nearly one full work week (or vacation week) for every
  traveler.[31]

When asked about their reaction to spending extra time
in their vehicles due to congestion delays, some motorists
responded that they enjoyed the solitary time with the ability to
listen to music, organize their thoughts, and so on. So if the personal statistics don't *get you*, the national statistics should. The

2.8 billion gallons of wasted fuel represents money that is being paid to foreign suppliers. It has a direct impact on our balance of payments and our economy. The wasted time of 4.2 billion hours is a drag on worker productivity. Time spent idling in traffic could be used productively to support U.S. commerce. These are significant numbers that are negatively influencing the economic health and global competitiveness of the United States.

So it's time for the transformation of the transportation system into a facility that meets the needs of the twenty-first century. Before exploring remedial prescriptions, it is important to understand the root causes that created these problems in the first place.

The State of the Highway System

Planning for an outer beltway in the Washington, DC region began during the 1950s with the recognition that circumferential traffic in the Washington, DC suburbs would eventually exceed the capacity of roadways currently planned or under construction. After decades of litigation, construction of this roadway began in 2007, nearly fifty years after the initial need for this facility was recognized. Motorists have been denied the availability of this facility, which eventually became known as the Intercounty Connector (the ICC), during the intervening years while transportation agencies struggled with bureaucratic and legal issues that must be followed to ensure the support of a majority of the public. The issues associated with this fifty-year-old project are representative of those that have delayed or prevented the addition of sorely needed capacity to the highway system.

And so a perfect storm has emerged within the highway transportation field created by three mutually reinforcing negative developments:

- Increasing travel demand without equivalent increase in supply of transportation services and infrastructure
- Inadequate funding to provide the needed supply of transportation facilities (new roadways)
- Growing opposition to desperately needed new supply

Thus, highway agencies are unable to respond to increasing demand from travelers and shippers for expanded transportation capacity.

Supply-Demand Imbalances

Economics students begin by learning the fundamental (and probably overly simplistic) relationship between supply and demand: Consumers purchase less of a given product as its price increases. At the same time, manufacturers will produce more of a given product if they can sell it at a higher price. The price at which the quantity of products produced equals the quantity of products purchased is called the equilibrium point. This concept is shown graphically in Figure 2. Thus, if you were the president of American Airlines during the great recession of 2008-09, you would have experienced a decrease in demand for airline travel. In response to the reduced demand, you would decrease the cost of airline seats with the anticipation that it would lead to increased demand. This is an interesting analogy to the roadway system since American Airlines can readily reduce its capacity by eliminating flights and, if needed, moth balling their older planes. However, increased capacity is difficult to achieve. So American Airlines ability to control demand is through its fare-pricing strategies. In this way, they can balance the demand for their product for compatibility with the capacity of their flights (supply), as well as the expectations of their investors. Operators of the highway system do not have the luxury of changing the cost of using roadway systems to achieve a balance between supply and demand.

Demand and supply relationships are important to the highway transportation industry. Demand is managed both explicitly and implicitly through the pricing of the product and the availability of transportation services. Travel demand is expressed in terms of vehicle miles of travel (VMT). If travel using public transportation (bus or rail) is being considered, travel demand is expressed in terms of person miles of travel (PMT). Supply is expressed in terms of lane miles of roadway. Cost or price is measured in terms of the monetary cost of the trip (fuel, vehicle

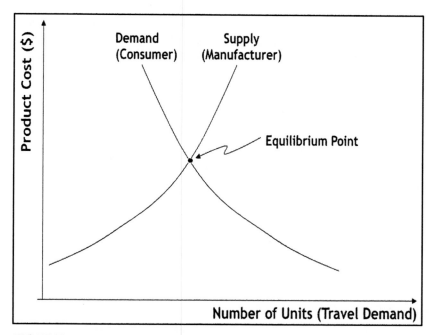

FIGURE 2 Supply-Demand Relationships

wear and tear, and the value of the traveler or shippers time). Cost may also be measured in less tangible terms using travel time or overall quality of the travel experience. Increasing congestion is the most obvious symptom of the misalignment of supply and demand.

These relationships can become complex, but they're worth understanding if legitimate solutions to the system's problems are to be identified. For example, when supply exceeds demand, travel is easy and relatively inexpensive. As indicated by the demand curve in Figure 2, lower travel costs means higher travel demand. This is good in terms of quality of life in that it provides the ability to readily travel whenever and wherever desired. However, it may be bad from a societal point of view since it means greater oil imports and increased pollution associated with greater travel demand.

When supply is less than demand, travel becomes expensive due to the time spent traveling (as the saying goes—time is money), wear and tear on the automobile or truck doing the traveling, and the cost of fuel. As travel becomes more expensive, fewer people travel. In other words, discretionary trips are eliminated. This relationship is demonstrated every time there is a sudden increase in gasoline prices when the public decides to postpone discretionary travel (usually vacation trips).

Unfortunately, the transportation industry does not have complete control over the pricing of its products and services. The cost of travel is determined by numerous suppliers, including the Organization of Petroleum Exporting Countries (OPEC), the oil companies, toll authorities, parking lot operators, transit companies, vehicle manufacturers, truckers, and railroads.

At least as far as the highway system is concerned, the industry also has little control over supply. As demonstrated by the ICC example, creation of new highway supply is a glacial process, in which the construction of new roadways can be delayed by thirty, forty, or even fifty years. Classical economic theory uses models of supply and demand, in which the demand decreases when the price increases, and price increases when there is a shortage of supply—usually without delay. These simplistic models are only partially applicable to the transportation system that is influenced by many societal factors other than simple supply/demand relationships. While some travel (demand) is discretionary, most trips are not. People travel in order to commute to work, shop, take their children to school and after-school activities, and attend business meetings. Truckers travel to move goods to market and to support manufacturing and farming activities. These combinations of discretionary and non-discretionary personal travel and freight movement lead to a continuing growth in demand that is generally unrelated to travel cost. In other words, simple models can't be used to represent the economics of the transportation system.

The Death Spiral of Additional Supply— Just Increases the Demand

Obviously, transportation demand associated with commuting is one of the greatest contributors to roadway congestion. It is only necessary to observe the increased traffic during the morning and evening hours to recognize this contribution. Numerous studies have evaluated the factors that impact commuting distance (race, sex, economic strata, etc.) and to no one's surprise have concluded that housing costs are the single most influential consideration. One such study was conducted by the Urban Land Institute whose report stated that:

> To find affordable homes, many in the workforce have followed the popular advice to drive till you qualify by moving to remote suburbs such as Warren and Fauquier counties, VA in the west; Spotsylvania County, VA and Charles County, MD in the south; Frederick County in the north; and Calvert County, MD in the east. As reflected in this report, however, efforts to save on housing expenses often lead to higher transportation costs, with the result that an even larger portion of household budgets are consumed by the combined burden of housing and transportation costs.[32]

As housing prices increase faster than salaries, families are forced to increase their commuting distance, with the cumulative impact of increased congestion, degraded air quality, and requirements for expansion of existing transportation infrastructure. The escalating societal costs associated with the expansion of suburbia and its related increase in commuting distance cannot continue. In other words, the American dream of home ownership in the suburbs may become a national and personal nightmare. So in addition to managing the travel costs, travel demand can be controlled by providing higher-density or lower-cost housing near employment centers.

The relative growth in supply and demand is shown graphically in the Figure 3. Within twenty-five years, supply increased 6 percent while demand increased 96 percent (nearly doubled). In other words, demand is significantly outpacing supply with no end in sight. If you think the roads are congested today, wait another ten years. The impact of the congestion resulting from this imbalance in supply and demand will be significantly greater travel costs for personal travelers and shippers alike, resulting from higher labor costs, increased vehicle wear and tear, and increased fuel costs. If it hasn't occurred already, it is likely that these increased costs will become a drag on the U.S. economy, leading to an environment in which the country will be less competitive in world markets. The reader is encouraged to commit these growth estimates to memory since they embody the transportation catastrophe that is waiting for future generations if nothing is done.

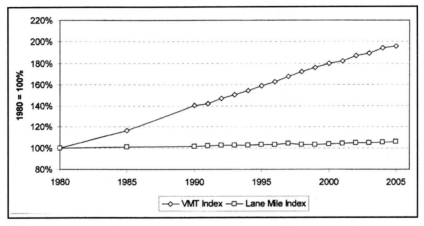

FIGURE 3 Comparison of Growth in Demand and Supply

Funding—Where is the Money Coming From?

The nation's highway programs are about to run out of money. AASHTO predicted that by 2009 income from fuel taxes and all other sources would be inadequate for routine maintenance of the highway system and existing commitments for new construction. This has lead to a debate between those who are automatically opposed to all tax increases and who feel that the problem is caused by inefficient use of existing money versus those who feel that transportation funding is essential to the nation's economic well-being.

To participate intelligently in the debate related to the future of the transportation system, it is important to understand the manner in which funds are received and disbursed. The primary source of highway transportation funding is the tax that is paid by motorists at the gas pump. You pay 18¢ in federal taxes for very gallon you put in your car. Additional state taxes range from 8¢ in Alaska (where fuel is subsidized) to 35.1¢ in Hawaii, for an average of 23.6¢ per gallon. When these costs are added to the federal tax, the average payment is 41.6¢ per gallon. Assuming you are paying $3.00 per gallon for your gas, the taxes you pay are approximately 14 percent of the total purchase. This is more than you would pay in state sales taxes for other products, but let's see what you receive for your 41.6¢ investment. "Suppose you own a car that gets twenty miles to the gallon, and you drive 16,000 miles per year. If this were the case, you would purchase eight hundred gallons of gas per year and pay an average of $333 per year in gas taxes. Assuming 100 percent of your gas taxes were used for new construction, as opposed to roadway and bridge maintenance, inspection, mowing, management of the system, and so on, your $333 in taxes would purchase a mere two inches of new roadway."[33] In other words, your gas tax payments have an imperceptible impact on the supply of available roadways.

However your $333 is not only used for new highway construction. An increasing percent of this money is used to pay for maintenance and replacement of the crumbling system that we currently use. Since the interstate system was built more than fifty years ago, it is not surprising that extensive maintenance (and in some cases reconstruction) is needed. Many other roadways throughout the United States are even older. Following the I-35W bridge collapse in Minneapolis, *USA Today* reported the results of a Gallup Poll that indicated that 67 percent of Americans are concerned about the safety of the bridges they use.[34] While these concerns are well placed, they are typically short-lived. For example, how many readers of this book even remember the collapse? As the news of the bridge collapse fades and Americans turn their attention to other aspects of their daily lives, concerns about the highway system evaporate. But those responsible for the safety of the highway system cannot forget about its deteriorating state. Maintenance costs take a 30 percent bite out of highway revenue, which means that approximately $100 of your $333 is diverted from new construction, or in other words, your tax payment actually purchases only 1.4 inches of new roadway.

How can there be a funding shortage when travel and gasoline usage is increasing? The problem is that usage isn't increasing nearly rapidly enough to make up for needed funding increases resulting from inflation and the continuing deterioration of the existing highway infrastructure. Furthermore, the rate of increase in fuel usage, which historically have counteracted the effects of inflation, have slowed considerably due to higher fuel prices and the introduction of more fuel-efficient cars. In other words, the assumption on which the gas tax is based (that increases in gasoline usage would offset the impacts of inflation) is no longer true. In fact, it hasn't been true for many years, which explains the supply-demand disparities that were presented earlier. But in 2009, the buzzards came home to roost! There were not adequate funds for any new construction. Thus, the second element of the perfect storm is one that cannot be ignored.

Opposition to New Construction

Some feel that the third element of the perfect storm is an example of democracy run amok. In its efforts to appease a myriad of factions who oppose construction of new facilities for numerous reasons (both justified and unjustified), a planning and design process has evolved that significantly increases the time and cost of new facilities and, in some cases, eliminates the possibility of their construction. The opposition may include a mix of community activists, local residents, environmentalists, bicyclists, pedestrians, local residents, transit supporters, truckers, various commercial interests, and sometimes even equestrians.

The ICC is an extreme, but not isolated, example of the degree to which the determined opposition can either defeat or delay the will of the majority as it relates to the construction of a new roadway. The original need for a facility of this nature was identified during the 1950s, with construction beginning in the fall of 2007, some fifty years later. The delays encountered by the ICC were the result of legal obstacles created by a coalition of environmentalists and community activists concerned that the roadway would do little to alleviate existing traffic congestion. They felt that the new roadway would generate additional development with its associated traffic, leading to further degradation of the environment, reduction in open space, and noise for the neighbors. These arguments, which may in fact be correct, are encountered prior to the construction of all new roadways but are particularly severe in the affluent suburbs of an already congested metropolitan area.

The process followed prior to the construction of the ICC is representative of the steps required for all new highway construction. This process is an alphabet soup of acronyms, reports, and analyses that is only understood by a small community of highway planners, engineers and regulators, and consultants. This group of specialists is responsible for ensuring that all the T's are crossed and the I's dotted in connection with the acquisition of federal approval and surviving court challenges associated with a new roadway. If things go smoothly, this process should require ONLY TWELVE years for the completion of major projects.[35] While a detailed description is beyond the intent of this book, the extent of the process can be appreciated by scanning the list of required studies and documentation, which include:

- For regional planning purposes
  —Unified planning work program
  —Twenty-year constrained long-range plan (CLRP)
  —Transportation improvement program (TIP)
  —Statewide transportation improvement program (STIP) which incorporates the TIPs
  —Environmental planning which includes, among other things an environmental assessment (EA), an environmental impact study (EIS), performed in accordance with the National Environmental Policy Act (NEPA).
- When the planning is completed, authorization for final design is applied for and received, a process that requires one year.

- In addition to final design, authorization for right-of-way acquisitions is applied for and received, a two-year process.
- Finally, authorization is received for construction, based on the final design and a refined cost estimate.
- Project construction begins, with completion anticipated twelve years after the beginning of the planning cycle.

This schedule assumes that the required funding is available and there are no court challenges. It also assumes that there are no unexpected delays experienced during the early phases of construction, such as the discovery of archeological artifacts, old cemeteries, or prehistoric remains, all of which could significantly slow or end the progress of a highway project.

One interesting example of unexpected difficulties encountered during highway construction can be found with a project in east Tennessee, whose objective was the widening of State Route 75 east of I-26 near the small town of Gray, Tennessee. In May 2000, workmen preparing the land for widening noticed a discoloration in the land. The discoloration proved to be a major fossil site containing hundreds of animal specimens from 4.5 million to 7.0 million years ago. This rare fossil site, which covers more than four acres, is the only one ever found in the Appalachian Mountains. As a result of its discovery, the right-of-way originally intended for Route 75 now houses a museum and a major excavation site. The redesigned roadway, whose widening was delayed by several years, now includes a gentle curve to avoid the site a, delay of several years.

Construction or widening of roadways is very disruptive, including changes to the environment, relocations, and dirt and noise—the end result of which is additional traffic. So the predicament of those responsible for providing high-quality transportation facilities for the American public is that the arguments of their opponents are frequently correct. New roads may in fact cause additional traffic, fuel consumption, and emissions. The question to be answered by the public at large, rather than a limited number of special interests, is whether the positive impact of a new road is worth the cost of the additional traffic it generates. Perhaps a more significant question is whether the relative desirability of a new road should be debated within a public forum as a democratic process or whether it should be part of the normal supply-demand relationships that are found in other aspects of our life, such as the demand for cellular telephone service and fuel oil, which are priced and supplied with minimal government intervention. In this latter case, the public votes with its pocketbook, rather than settling differences through the courts. Thus, there is an implicit question in this third element of the perfect storm—how do we balance the competing forces of the transportation equation: as part of a democratic process, or by reliance on the self-correcting forces of the commercial marketplace?

This is not a hypothetical question. The three elements of the perfect storm must be addressed and resolved if we are to maintain our current high standard of living and remain competitive within world markets. In other words, a system that met the promises of the twentieth century must be translated into a system that meets the needs of the twenty-first century. There are some who feel that the only way in which these needs can be met is through a massive restructuring of the manner in which transportation services are being delivered. More about this later.

CHAPTER 4

Getting There Alive

Every closed eye is not sleeping, and every open eye is not seeing.

—Bill Cosby[36]

~~~~~~

ON SEPTEMBER 19, 2006, MSNBC REPORTED THAT A serious E. coli outbreak linked to spinach had occurred in the United States. The report indicated that one (possibly two) deaths were being investigated by federal officials. Ultimately, three unfortunate souls succumbed to the E. coli bacteria, an event that was covered by all of the major media outlets. During the two-month period that the *spinach problem* was receiving elevated attention, approximately 7,200 individuals died in automobile accidents within the United States and 200,000 died worldwide without any media attention. So congestion is not the only problem associated with the nation's highway system. Unsafe roads are another significant issue. Have we become desensitized to automobile fatalities since they are so frequent?

While even a single fatality is not to be taken lightly, the statistics of highway death and destruction defy comparisons with the impacts of E. coli bacteria. In fact, they even defy comparisons with the effects of war and starvation. As shown in Table 1, the World Health Organization (WHO) reports that over the past ten years the worldwide life-shortening consequences of automobile accidents have risen from ninth place to third place, ahead of war (eighth place) and HIV (tenth place).[37] Rankings in this table are measured in terms of disability adjusted life year (DALY), which is a measure that combines information on the number of years lost from premature death with the loss of health from disability.

1990		2000	
Rank	**Disease**	**Rank**	**Disease**
1	Lower Respiratory Infections	1	Ischaemic heart disease
2	Diarrheal diseases	2	Unipolar major depression
3	Perinatal conditions	3	Road traffic injuries
4	Unipolar major depression	4	Cerebrovascular disease
5	Ischaemic heart disease	5	Chronic obstructive pulmonary disease
6	Cerebrovascular disease	6	Lower Respiratory Infections
7	Tuberculosis	7	Tuberculosis
8	Measles	8	War
9	Road traffic injuries	9	Diarrheal diseases
10	Congenital abnormalities	10	HIV

TABLE 1   Rank of 10 Leading Causes of Global Burden of Disease

Consider the statistics: In 2005, there were more than 43,000 auto-related fatalities in the United States and nearly 1.2 million fatalities worldwide annually. The number of injuries in auto accidents is equally staggering with nearly 40 million injured worldwide.

A pandemic is defined as "an epidemic over a wide geographic area and affecting a large proportion of the population." Clearly because of the worldwide death and injury rates, auto safety can be considered a pandemic. Yet the policy and investment emphasis placed on this pandemic by most governments worldwide is dwarfed by the focus on other life threatening concerns that often pose less serious societal problems.

The Pandemic Can be Cured

The most compelling evidence that solutions to the highway safety pandemic exist can be found in the safety initiatives successfully implemented in Victoria, Australia during the period of 1989 through 2004. Detailed descriptions of the Victoria program exist elsewhere and should be required reading for legislators as well as the general public since a program such as the one implemented by the Australians requires comprehensive policy support.[38]

The success of the Australian program is enviable. Since its inception, the fatality rate in Victoria has dropped from approximately 22.5 deaths per 100,000 population to nine deaths per 100,000 population, a decrease of 60 percent to just over half of the U.S. fatality rate. These impressive results were achieved through the combined support of public agency and political officials, with majority (although far from unanimous) public support for a comprehensive program that spanned the three Es of safety: education, enforcement, and engineering. The success of the program was further ensured through strong legislative support and ultimately, continuous performance measurement. This program deserves particular attention in the United States, since Australia, like the United States, is a "federation, but mostly because it is part of the 'new world' where urban form, regional development, and road transport developed more or less contemporaneously."[39]

Highlights of the Victoria program include:

- Legislation that increased police powers, increased penalties and clarified existing regulations. This legislation included a zero blood alcohol requirement, increase of the probationary license period from two to three years, compulsory helmets for bicyclists, and immediate license loss for second drunk driving offenses.
- Greatly increased speed enforcement including extensive use of speed photo enforcement
- Increased random breath testing for detection of drunk drivers by a factor of five. Statistically, this means that one in three drivers in Victoria can expect to be stopped each year.
- Introduced a long-term program of public education in support of specific safety initiatives, in order to maintain the visibility of traffic safety with the general public

In summary, three overall factors can be identified as having contributed to the success in Victoria:[40]

1. A sound and realistic plan (more about this later)
2. Political and bureaucratic leadership that recognizes that the enforcement and engineering cannot accomplish their goals without an underlying legislative mandate as well as adequate funding
3. Integrated implementation in which the three E's are used to complement each other

The Australian program is not alone in its successful improvement of highway safety. However, it provides an invaluable example of the potential benefits of a fully integrated program with a foundation of strong legislative support. Equally important, rather than expending resources chasing a large number of safety issues, the program focuses on the major causes of traffic fatalities: speed and alcohol.

A Focus on Speed and Drunk Driving

According to the National Highway Traffic Safety Administration (NHTSA), speed and drunk driving accounted for 30 percent and 40 percent of fatal crashes annually.[41] Obviously these percentages are not additive since approximately 40 percent of the fatal speed-related crashes involved drivers with blood alcohol concentrations (BACs) of .08 grams per deciliter (g/dL) or higher. Adjusting for this double counting, it can be concluded that taken together, speed and alcohol account for approximately 58 percent of the fatal crashes in the United States, and major reductions in these two areas alone will have a significant impact on highway fatalities. Obviously there are other potential focus areas for improvements that can be realized that include young drivers and pedestrians. Speed and alcohol also received the greatest emphasis in the Victoria program.

Speed

In the United States and elsewhere, there is a debate regarding the relative value of lower speed limits versus reduced speed variance (speed differentials among vehicles sharing the same roadway). While there is evidence to support the safety benefits of both, it goes without saying that existing fixed regulatory signing with unrealistic speed limits that are universally ignored by motorists have limited value. In most areas of the United States, the 55-mile-per-hour (mph) speed limit has, for all intents and purposes, produced a nation of law-breakers. On many U.S. roadways, it is common for nearly 100 percent of the vehicles to be exceeding the speed limit, a fact that calls into question the value of existing speed limit signage. There are three alternatives to the current situation:

1. Retain the 55-mph speed limits and greatly increase enforcement such that speeders are assured of receiving a citation. Photo enforcement or other automated enforcement techniques are the only way in which an appropriate intensity of enforcement can be practically achieved.

2. Increase speed limits to a level that reflects actual highway speeds. Combine the increased speed limits with increased concentration of enforcement. Safety advocates are likely to (correctly) oppose this measure, since *actual highway speeds* are variable depending on time of day, weather conditions, roadway geometrics, percent of familiar drivers, and vehicle mix (trucks versus autos). A higher speed that may be safe for one set of conditions could be unsafe under other conditions. However, unless the number of speed violators is significantly below 100 percent (and probably below 10 percent), manual enforcement techniques are impractical.

3. Take advantage of existing technology to implement a regulatory variable speed system in which speed limits are automatically displayed at the prevailing 85 percentile speeds, on the theory that the majority of drivers will automatically select the safe speed for prevailing traffic and roadway conditions. Here again, the variable speed limit must be accompanied by an intensified enforcement program. This approach is likely to produce the highest level of public acceptance for increased enforcement (including the use of automated techniques), since the perceived benefits of *sensible* speed limits will offset objections to the increased enforcement. Alternatives (2) and (3) require legislative actions.

The common denominator of these three techniques is greatly increased enforcement, which must be accompanied by an intense public education program explaining the benefits of the selected approach. As demonstrated by the Victoria program, whichever alternative is selected must be accompanied by legislative policy support and adequate funding to ensure its success. In this manner, the three Es of safety are employed. Any of these three alternatives is superior to the current sporadic enforcement of unrealistic speed limits.

Drunk Driving

The public recognizes the consequences of drunk driving to a much greater extent than speed and has supported increased penalties for those driving while intoxicated. This may be the result of the efforts of groups such as Mothers Against Drunk Drivers (MADD), or it could be caused by the fact that a relatively small percentage of motorists drive under the influence, while "everyone speeds." Whatever the reason, the penalties for driving under the influence (DUI) have been significantly increased during the past twenty years, with approximately 1,600 new DUI laws passed nationwide within the United States since 1980. A few examples include the fact that "all states have adopted 21 as the legal drinking age, and two-thirds of the states have passed administrative license revocation (ALR) laws, which allow the arresting officer to take the license of drivers who fail or refuse to take a breath test. In addition, many states have lowered the legal BAC limit from 0.10 to 0.08 percent for adults, and more than a dozen states have passed zero tolerance laws which prohibit drivers under 21 from having any measurable amount of alcohol in their blood system."[42]

But it is too early to declare victory. While these measures along with extensive public education are likely to be responsible for a nearly 5 percent reduction in alcohol related fatalities, this slow progress is unacceptable in view of the fact that more than 14,000 individuals lost their lives in 2005 due to drunk driving. It is clear that additional steps must be taken, again to include increased enforcement, expanded public education, and additional funding. A list of measures that have proven effective is presented on DUI.com, a website supported by the state of California.[43] A sample of the measures listed by this reference, over and above those that were previously mentioned, includes:

- Alcohol treatment programs
- Server intervention and education programs
- House arrest in lieu of jail
- Lower acceptable levels of BAC for repeat offenders
- Greatly increasing the number of sobriety checkpoints (as per the Victoria program)
- Expanded public information and education
- Effective vehicle-based countermeasures
- Vehicle impoundment or immobilization
- Ignition interlock

The referenced website indicates that measures being used that have not proven effective include jail or community service and fines, even though these approaches continue to be used.

Ignition interlocks are of particular interest, since they have been shown to reduce repeat offenses by 50 percent to 90 percent.[44] These devices operate by requiring the driver to breath into a device that determines the BAC level. If preset limits are exceeded, the vehicle will not start. Other forms of interlocks are on the horizon, including one in which the driver's BAC is measured by steering wheel sensors. These devices, which represent the engineering E, combined with aggressive enforcement and increased education, offer the promise of significant reductions in alcohol related fatalities.

Traffic Safety in the United States

The successes of the Australians and others, the availability of new technologies, and an improved understanding of the highway safety problem and its cures are all causes for optimism. The United States, as a leader in technology, with a well-funded safety research program should be a world leader in the field of highway safety.

Elected officials responsible for the funding and oversight of transportation agencies pay lip service to safety yet tolerate the continued operation of a highway system responsible for more than 43,000 fatalities per year. Think about it—43,000 deaths on the U.S. highway system each year exceeds the annual number of combat deaths the nation has experienced during any of the wars that took place during the twentieth and twenty-first centuries. This apathy toward the slaughter on the highways would be understandable if it were incurable—like cancer, AIDs, or even war. But the sad truth is that the highway death rate in the United States ranks fourteenth in a list of twenty-four highly developed countries. In other words, many other countries have at least found a partial cure for the highway fatality disease. In simple terms, the number of lives lost on highways every two years would be equivalent to the death of the entire population of the city of Olympia, Washington, a situation that would not be tolerated in any modern society. But shock statistics of this nature have been used for many years with no impact on the public or their elected officials. By far the most shocking of all is the fact that we have the tools to do something about it.

In 1998, the Federal Highway Administration (FHWA) published a strategic plan in which it established the goals of a 20 percent reduction in fatalities and a 20 percent reduction in serious injuries within ten years.[45] As indicated in Table 2, the United States is not only failing to meet these goals, but fatalities have continued to increase since the plan was published. The fatality rate decreased between 1998 and 2004 but with the exception of 2003 and 2004, the total number of fatalities consistently increased. The statistics for 2005 are particularly

NHTSA Fatality Data	2009	2008	2007	2006	2005	2004	2003	2002
Fatal Crashes	30,797	34,172	37,435	38,648	39,252	38,444	38,477	38,491
Total Fatalities	33,808	37,423	41,259	42,708	43,510	42,836	42,884	43,005
National Rates:								
Fatalities per 100 million Vehicle Miles Traveled	1.13	1.26	1.36	1.42	1.46	1.44	1.48	1.51
Fatalities per 100,000 Population	11.01	12.30	13.68	14.30	14.71	14.62	14.77	14.94
Fatalities per 100,000 Registered Vehicles	Not Available	17.96	20.05	21.06	21.70	21.54	21.86	22.10

TABLE 2   History of US Fatalities

alarming since both the number of fatalities and the fatality rate increased over those for 2004.

This lack of progress reduces the FHWA strategic plan to little more than a publicity piece since the results have so little relationship to the goals. During the eight years since the plan was announced, there has been little tracking of results and almost no mid-course corrections to ensure that the goals are being met. Perhaps most important there has been little legislative support for the use of techniques that will ensure these goals are met. There is little point in strategic planning without assurance of the needed underlying support.

To be effective, strategic plans must include the following characteristics:

- "The traffic safety problems to be addressed should be the major problems and each should be tractable.
- The action plan should include interventions for which there is adequate scientific evidence of likely effectiveness (or controlled trials of innovations of unknown effectiveness).
- The implementing agencies should have transparent lines of accountability for effective implementation."[46]

The FHWA strategic plan violates many of these guidelines in that it makes no attempt to identify the root causes of roadway injuries and fatalities and makes no connection between the strategies and the problem to be solved.

Speed and alcoholism are major highway safety problems. Yet there is demonstrated evidence that they are tractable. Many interventions with proven effectiveness exist, if only the United States and its counterparts throughout the world would adopt appropriate planning methodologies and muster the political will for their implementation. Unless the obvious steps are taken, the auto safety pandemic will continue with social consequences that dwarf the impacts of E. coli bacteria on lettuce, and for that matter, most major wars.

CHAPTER 5

Paying For the System—
Getting A Silk Purse From A Sow's Ear

*Everybody wants to eat at the government's
table, but nobody wants to do the dishes.*
—Werner Finck [47]

~~~~~~

BY NOW, YOU SHOULD BE PERSUADED THAT THE
nation's highway system suffers from inadequate capacity and
unacceptably high accident rates. There are many potential solutions to this problem, including the more effective operation of
the highway system and the application of advanced technology.
However, all of these solutions require funding (money), which
is in short supply as highway agencies struggle to repair and
reconstruct the crumbling highway system. Don't forget that
many of today's highways and bridges are more than fifty years
old, an age at which expensive rehabilitation is required if we
are to avoid losing our trillion-dollar investment.

At a recent social gathering, a friend asked me what I thought
about proposals to increase the gasoline tax. The answers to this
question can be complex since they require an understanding of
the impending financial crisis within the highway community,
as well as the mechanisms of the gasoline tax. With this in mind,
I tactfully (for me at least) preceded my response with some
probing questions in an effort to determine the questioner's
understanding of the basic issues associated with transportation

funding. The responses I received proved fascinating in that they revealed the extent of the misunderstandings that my friend, as well as most of the American public, have about government's responsibility for the construction, maintenance, and operations of the roads on which they travel. In other words, most people do not know who to blame for our increasing transportation difficulties. A few of these misconceptions and their associated truths include the following:

- Misconception: the federal government owns and operates the highway system (or at least the interstate system). Actually, nothing could be further from the truth. Although there are some variations, the states are generally responsible for the construction, operation, and maintenance of all interstate roadways and state routes. Counties and cities are responsible for neighborhood streets and other minor roadways in their jurisdiction. Have you ever seen a snow plow with a federal agency's name on it except in the national parks? Although it is not responsible for most roads, the federal government is involved with highway programs through the regulation and funding process.

- Misconception: congestion is so bad in urban areas that nothing can be done about it. Congestion is bad, but many jurisdictions could improve the operation of their roadways. There is a long list of potential improvements, many of which are discussed in later chapters. One example would be improved operation of traffic signals during congested periods to reduce the delays at congested intersections. Studies have shown that the simple act of improving traffic signal timing at all the intersections in the United States would save motorists more than 17 billion gallons of motor fuels per year.[48]

- Misconception: the United States operates the most technologically advanced highway system in the world. Travelers outside the United States have undoubtedly noticed effective applications of technology that is unavailable in the United States. One example of many are the displays of information regarding parking availability in many European cities, a technology that is virtually non-existent in the United States.

- Misconception: the United States operates the safest transportation system in the world. Table 3, which compares the U.S. auto death rate with a sample of western European countries, puts this misconception into perspective.[49] In fact, the United States is near the bottom of the list of fatalities when compared with highly developed European countries. While the data in this table is rather dated, the situation has not improved. The U.S. fatality rate has declined but more slowly than the fatality rate of the other countries in the table. In other words, these statistics are embarrassing and are certainly not representative of a twenty-first-century highway system.

Country	Number of Deaths per 100,000 Population
United Kingdom	3.4
Netherlands	4.1
Switzerland	4.7
Norway	5.4
Germany	5.5
Finland	6.5
France	6.9
Spain	6.9
Denmark	7.4
Ireland	7.8
Italy	8.7
Luxembourg	9.0
United States	12.3
Turkey	13.4
Greece	14.4

TABLE 3 Traffic-Related Death Rate by Country

- Misconception: if we give politicians additional money (e.g., pay higher gas taxes), they'll just waste it on more earmarks (also known as pork barrel projects) such as the infamous Alaskan bridge to nowhere. There is no denying the fact that large funding programs attract political earmarks. However, one person's wasteful pork barrel project is another person's fulfillment of a critical need, including beneficial local employment. Dubious earmarks are not unique to the highway industry. They are found in healthcare, education, and defense spending, with the latter being the biggest. Just as we should not consider major reductions in national defense spending due to the existence of earmarks, we must not use these earmarks as an excuse to reduce funding for highway bridge inspections. The earmark problem should be solved without using it as an excuse to starve a critical program.

The one thing that should be clear to the general public is that highway agencies do not have complete control over the pricing of their products and services. The cost of travel is determined by numerous public and private sector organizations, including OPEC, the oil companies, toll authorities, parking lot operators, transit companies, vehicle manufacturers, truckers, and railroads.

The extent of the existing funding crisis was captured recently by a recent FOX News interview with representatives of the Georgia Department of Transportation.[50]

"As the recession threatens popular highway programs, the Georgia Department of Transportation is looking to the private sector for creative funding solutions."

"Necessity is the mother of invention," said Georgia DOT Spokesman David Spear. "If we're not broke, we're as close as we want to get to it. And we've got to find ways to maximize our resources.

"Now, advertising revenue covers nearly all of Georgia's costs involved with its federally subsidized highway assistance program in Metro Atlanta. State Farm Insurance pays the Georgia DOT $1.7 million a year to have its company logo placed on the state's eighty-six highway emergency response operator vehicles, or HERO units. Drivers of the bright yellow trucks assist drivers, getting their stranded vehicles out of the way of busy traffic by filling empty tanks or changing tires.

"Other corporate sponsors cover the $500,000 annual cost of Georgia's 511 traffic information program. And the state has started making money by outsourcing logo signs, which announce food, lodging, gas stations, and local attractions at highway exits—a program the DOT had operated at a loss on its own.

"We brought in a private sector partner in that, quite frankly, knows how to do this considerably better than we did," Spear said. "They're making money. We're making money.

"What's happening in Georgia is part of a national trend, as cash-strapped highway departments search for new sources of revenue without raising taxes."

Obviously it is difficult to criticize those responsible for the construction, maintenance, and operation of the nation's highway system when they are struggling to obtain the funding needed to ensure its safe and efficient operation. After all, the availability of adequate funding is essential to providing a system capable of sustaining the nation's continued growth and vitality. As you read the following description of alternative funding sources, consider the fact that our political system is designed to reward failure. In other words, the greater the level of congestion and higher accident rates, the more funding received. Transportation is often ranked among the top ten concerns of voters. It has only moved into this position within the past decade. This would not be the case if we did not have congested roadways, thousands of fatal accidents, and collapsing bridges. These dire situations ensure the continuing flow of scarce federal and state funding into the improvement of the transportation infrastructure. The problem is that the system used to finance the highway system is currently broken, and new approaches will be needed to provide the needed money.

Where Does the Money Come From?

To participate intelligently in the debate of funding for highways, it is important to understand the manner in which funds are currently received and disbursed. But it is equally important to appreciate the return that the nation receives from its investment.

Benefits of the Highway Investment

If you were the CEO of a major corporation and had surplus cash that could be invested in various ways, you would decide how to spend this money (at least in part) based on the alternative that offered the greatest rate of return on the expenditure. Hypothetically, suppose you were in charge of the XYZ Widget Company, and you had $10 million in the bank that was providing a very modest income based on a 1 percent annual interest rate. Surely this money could be used more wisely, providing the company's owners with a better return on their investment. In other words, the rate of return received for the $10-million bank deposit is certainly not great. As the CEO, you authorize a search of various companies that are currently for sale, which might include a rubber band manufacturer whose rate of return on a $10-million investment would be 7 percent and a ballpoint pen manufacturer offering a rate of return of 4 percent. You also compare these possibilities with corporate bonds offering a rate of return of 8 percent. As a result of this comparison, you would probably decide to invest the $10 million in corporate bonds, which offer a higher rate of return. Of course this decision would have to be balanced against the potential for future growth, risk, and myriad other factors.

Public sector investments are not usually compared with private sector investments using the rate of return concept because of the difficulty of calculating the financial returns of these public investments that are often received in the form of social benefits. However, some brave souls have attempted to calculate the rate of return for highway investments because of the obvious payback in terms of their impact on both the manufacturing and services industries. If sales people can reduce the travel time between calls, their productivity is improved because they can make more calls. If the time (and hence the cost) of shipping raw materials to factories and goods to markets is decreased, the cost of producing these goods is decreased with the resulting improved profitability of the producer.

While these concepts appear simple, in practice they can become quite complex due to the many different types of roadways and the numerous activities they impact. However, as summarized in a report prepared by the Delcan Corporation, the rate of return can and has been calculated with some astonishing results that include:[51]

- During the period of 1960 though 1990, the rate of return for investment in highways (an astounding 32 percent) was nearly double the average for private markets during the same period
- The studies reviewed showed that every economic sector of the United States experienced significant benefits from highway investment. Surprisingly, the greatest gains were in the service sector, which is counter-intuitive since the benefits of highway system improvements to the trucking industry are the most obvious.
- Improvements in the highway system expanded the private sector's ability to access markets and labor. As a result, the efficiency of most industries increased with the potential for increased profitability and growth.

These facts are not hypothetical. They provide demonstrated evidence of the value of spending money on highways because of the significant return that the nation receives on its public investment. The question addressed here is the manner in which this investment can be made in a politically acceptable manner.

Finding the Money

In Chapter 3, the fact that fuel usage isn't increasing nearly rapidly enough to make up for increases in construction costs was described. Things became even worse during the 2008-2009 recession during which travel decreased significantly, further aggravating the funding situation. Gasoline usage has also been slowed by higher fuel prices and the introduction of more fuel-efficient cars and hybrid vehicles. The assumption that increases in gasoline usage would offset the impacts of inflation is no longer true. If it were not for an infusion of money from the general fund (that is where your tax dollars go) and stimulus funding (provided in an effort to reverse the impacts of the recession), new highway construction and maintenance would have come to a complete halt. The American Society of Civil Engineers (ASCE) has estimated that highway funding from all sources must be increased by 42 percent to a total investment of $92 billion just to maintain the status quo.[52] This appears to be a significant amount of money until it is put in perspective. The 42 percent increase would require the gas tax to be raised from an average of 42¢ per gallon (including both federal and state taxes) to approximately 60¢ per gallon, an amount that is dwarfed by the taxes paid by Europeans. For example, the gas tax in England is approximately $4.00 per gallon versus 42¢ per gallon, or nearly ten times higher.

Solving the Problem

Obviously maintaining the status quo is not an option. In spite of the opposition of those who automatically oppose all attempts to increase revenue for any purpose, it is clear that something must be done. If maintenance activities are not accelerated, we are in danger of losing the trillion-dollar investment in our nation's highway system due to its deterioration. If the pace of construction of new facilities is not increased, the supply of new roadways will increasingly lag behind the rapid increases in demand that can be anticipated as the recession comes to an end. If we do not take advantage of the benefits of advanced technology, our roadways will continue to be utilized inefficiently. In all cases, our economy and safety will suffer.

There are many potential solutions to the problem, many of which are receiving serious consideration and some of which are being demonstrated or implemented in the United States and other locations throughout the world.

Increase the Gas Tax

The most obvious approach to raising the money needed to support the nation's highway system is to increase the gas tax. AASHTO has suggested that one such approach would be to replace the current flat 18¢ per gallon tax with a sales tax of 8.4 percent. This figure was calculated to avoid any immediate increase in tax payments by motorists but with the anticipation that revenue will increase with increasing fuel prices. While this proposal appears to solve the problem, it must be considered a temporary Band-Aid. Increasing fuel efficiency and the likelihood of significant increases in the number of hybrid and all-electric cars will hopefully reduce the use of gasoline for transportation purposes. As a result, we will be again faced with another financial emergency as revenues decline due to reduced gasoline usage.

But even this proposal, which should have little impact on the public, is likely to be dead on arrival. The current anti-tax political climate verges on the irrational considering that the need is intense and the impact of the proposed change in the gas tax mechanism is modest. Legislators have consistently expressed concern about the impact of a gas tax increase on low-income travelers and the economy overall. These arguments existed when gas was under $2 per gallon. Since that time, prices have increased by more than 50¢ per gallon without any measurable impacts on the economy. In fact, the only observable impact was to increase the public's short-term interest in purchasing hybrids and more fuel-efficient vehicles. So why should we be concerned about a revenue neutral sales tax, or as suggested above, an 18¢ increase in the gas tax? If we are honest with ourselves, to quote Pogo, "we have met the enemy and they are us." Politicians have attached the label of socialism and ultra-liberalism to any proposal that carries the dirty word *taxes* or worse yet *tax increase*. As a result, our legislators are running for cover, and the prospects for a gas tax increase are very dim.

These thoughts were expressed by Ray LaHood, secretary of the U.S. Department of Transportation, when he indicated in a recent speech before AASHTO that increases in the gas tax are dead on arrival and that those who are proposing these increases do not have to face the public. He added that the Obama administration recently is not prepared to suggest fuel tax increases in a time of high unemployment and national resistance to tax increases of any kind. So it is time to look at other sources of revenue if our existing infrastructure is to be saved and problems of congestion and safety are to be addressed—sources of revenue that do not contain the dreaded T word but offer the same end result of charging highway users for their use of these invaluable roadway facilities.

Toll Roads and Other Pricing Schemes

Toll roads are certainly not new. Chapter 1 describes the private toll roads that were in operation during the late eighteenth century, continuing into the nineteenth century. The Pennsylvania Turnpike is one of the earliest examples of a modern publicly owned toll road. Since that time, tolling has become popular for turnpikes, tunnels, and bridges. The toll facilities of the twenty-first century are quite different from those of the 1800s. Although the roads of both centuries received their revenue in the form of tolls, the modern roads, bridges, and tunnels collect their tolls electronically utilizing electronic toll payment through interaction with equipment mounted in the car. EZPass and SunPass are two examples of electronic toll payment. In many facilities, and most new facilities, tolls are collected without the use of tollbooths. Motorists' accounts are debited as they pass electronic readers at highway speeds, eliminating the delays associated with the payment of tolls and the cost of personnel involved in the process. This latter technique is known as open road tolling.

In some cases, toll lanes may be added to an existing free roadway where tolls are collected from all vehicles except those with more than a predetermined number of passengers, designated high-occupancy vehicles (HOVs). The HOVs are permitted to use the lanes at no cost. A new acronym has been created from the joint designation of HOV and toll lanes, which are known as HOT lanes. HOT lanes are being added to the capital beltway (I-495) in northern Virginia. The toll rates for use of the northern Virginia facility vary with traffic conditions.

As congestion on the lane increases, the toll paid also increases with the objective of discouraging people from using the lane. In this way, the operator of the lane can reduce demand during congested conditions in order to provide a guaranteed quality of service. This pricing strategy is known as congestion pricing, value pricing, or variable pricing. The term value pricing was recently coined by the U.S. Department of Transportation in an effort to make the concept of charging for service more palatable to the public and to avoid the use of the dreaded T word.

Congestion pricing is not only applied to freeways. It is being used to control traffic entering congested city centers. This approach is being used in Singapore, London, and a number of smaller urban areas. Although congestion pricing has been implemented on a number of freeways in the United States, it has yet to be applied to urban areas. It is important to recognize that the primary purpose of this technique is to improve traffic flow and reduce vehicular emissions, rather than raising revenue. However, these systems have been shown to generate significant revenue. In some urban areas, a portion of the tolls are used to provide improved transit service.

So imagine a world in which gas taxes remain unrealistically low or disappear completely but one in which you are charged a toll wherever you travel. This concept is not as new or as strange as you might think. Isn't that what happens every time you ride on a plane, bus, or train? The fees charged for many of these services are set to minimize congestion. If you doubt this, try to purchase an airline ticket for the day before Thanksgiving. You are being charged for the delivery of a transportation service whose value changes with the demand for the service. The power of this concept is that it gives the supplier (highway owners and operators) the ability to influence the behavior of the traveler. By raising or lowering tolls, the supplier can encourage off-peak travel or travel on underutilized roadways. Appropriately setting the toll rates can also be used to encourage the use of transit.

VMT Pricing

A relatively new financing scheme has emerged that is receiving serious consideration from policy makers and some elected officials. Known as VMT (vehicle miles traveled) pricing, this scheme replaces the gas tax with a charge based on the number of miles traveled. At first glance, this appears to be a very attractive alternative to the gas price since motorists would be charged based on the amount of travel rather than the amount of gasoline consumed by their vehicle. VMT pricing also offers the significant advantage that it is unaffected by the introduction of hybrids or electric vehicles since the income to the government is based on miles traveled rather than the quantity of gasoline used to get there. However, this is a double-edged sword since it eliminates some of the government's ability to encourage the purchase of fuel-efficient vehicles through the imposition of very high gasoline taxes and lower electricity costs. After all, this is what has occurred in Europe, where extremely high gas taxes have led to the purchase of significantly smaller and more fuel-efficient vehicles.

There is another drawback to VMT pricing: the need for the government to keep track of the number of miles driven by each vehicle, a requirement that would require the installation of monitoring devices in every vehicle in the country that would record the number of miles you travel. Proposals for advanced versions of this pricing scheme have included the enhancement of the monitoring devices to include the ability to track when and where you travel so that you can be charged a higher rate for trips made during congested periods of the day or in congested areas. This is very appealing to the operators of the transportation system, since like congestion pricing, they can influence the travel behavior of the public with the end result of improving conditions in severely congested areas.

But will VMT pricing ever be accepted by the public and its elected officials? Consider the privacy advocates who worry about providing the government with the ability to track its citizens. Consider the anti-tax advocates who will see this as another underhanded way to squeeze more money out of the public. The enemies of this scheme are likely to be legion.

As if concerns about privacy and hidden taxes were not enough, the cost of equipping all of the 250 million cars in the

United States with devices capable of measuring miles traveled as a function of time and location is indeed daunting. Even if the cost of the mileage recording devices were less than $50, the total cost to the nation would be $2.45 billion.

And that's not all. This scheme also requires the installation of facilities to read the mileage recorded by each vehicle. One proposal is to equip gas stations with readers that can be used by motorists to pay their mileage fees. There are more than 130,000 gas stations in the United States. Assuming that the cost of the equipment as well as its installation is $5,000 per station, the total additional cost of the VMT pricing system would be increased by an additional $650 million, raising the total price of implementing VMT pricing to more than $3 billion, a cost that the public is likely to reject.

Private Sector Participation

Many transportation agencies have turned to the private sector as a source of badly needed funding. Toll roads constructed by the private sector as an investment opportunity appear to offer the greatest promise. You may recall from Chapter 1 that this is not a new discovery. Private toll roads were popular during the late 1700s and early 1800s. You might also recall from Chapter 1 that the popularity of these roads waned due to technology failures (the corduroy roads deteriorated more quickly than anticipated), competition from alternative forms of transportation (railroads), burdensome regulation, and low rates of return to investors. The same ingredients for failure are very much alive for the twenty-first-century highway. Ironically, with the rush to embrace the construction of roads at no cost to the government, one rarely hears the current situation compared with the pitfalls of the nineteenth century.

But in spite of the risk, the income or cost savings from private sector participation in highway construction and operation can be substantial. For example, the HOT lanes in northern Virginia, described earlier in this chapter, will cost nearly $2 billion. This level of investment could not possibly have made by the Virginia Department of Transportation (VDOT). In short, the HOT lanes would not have been constructed without the investment of Transurban, VDOT's private sector partner.

As demonstrated by the FOX News quotation describing Georgia's activities, private sector funding is available from other sources beside toll roads. While Georgia has focused on advertising revenue, other approaches have been used, such as sharing their communications facilities with the private sector, providing private sector access to public right of way for construction of cell phone towers, installation of privately owned fiber optic cable on public right of way, and allowing advertising on public sector facilities such as service patrol vehicles and websites.

Public-private partnerships can be a tricky business because of the cultural difference between the two types of organizations as well as their different objectives. Public transportation agencies tend to be conservative and risk averse. They tend to approach partnership opportunities cautiously and in their attempts to protect the public good, often impose terms and conditions on these partnerships, which at best restrict the potential return on the private sector investment and at worst cause the failure of the investment.

The private sector is focused on the profitability of the enterprise. While there may be altruistic motives attached to the project, in almost all cases, the project must be profitable to succeed. The private sector has the benefit of increased flexibility in terms of its employment practices (salaries, promotions, hiring, firing, working hours, etc.) and can acquire equipment and services without requiring competitive procurements. Thus, the private sector is fundamentally more agile than the public sector and can potentially complete a project more efficiently than could be achieved by a public sector organization.

It would appear that all transportation projects would benefit from private sector participation. However, the danger of this approach is the difficulty of regulating private sector performance and the inability of the contracting agency to ensure that unprofitable services such as transit are provided. Perhaps the greatest risk is that the private company will abandon a particular project if required levels of profitability are not achieved, as demonstrated by the experiences of the nineteenth century. To a certain extent, these difficulties can be overcome through appropriate contract requirements, unless the lack of profitability causes the failure of the private company behind the project. In such a case, the responsible public agency is left *holding the bag*. This occurred in the state of Washington whose residents had come to rely on the Puget Sound Navigation Company for ferry service on Puget Sound in the Seattle region. During the 1940s, when labor unions successfully negotiated a salary increase, the Puget Sound Navigation Company petitioned the state for a 30 percent fare increase. When their petition was denied, the company tied up its ferries and abandoned the service. The state was forced to purchase the ferries and other facilities and establish the Washington State Ferries Authority to ensure the continued provision of the service. Thus, the taxpayers paid for a private-sector failure. Public-private partnerships can be a mixed blessing.

Funding the Twenty-First-Century Highway System

So how do we fund the transformation of the twentieth-century highway system into one that is suitable for the twenty-first century? There is little doubt that significant resources will be needed if we are to avoid a degraded quality of life and a hobbled economy. The solution is likely to involve a combination of increased fuel taxes (in spite of the dislike of that concept), increased private sector participation, and money paid from the federal government's general fund. It appears that the days of a dedicated stream of revenue exclusively from the gas tax are gone. The highway industry will have to learn how to effectively make its case for adequate funding to federal and state legislatures in an era of heavy competition from other governmental agencies and functions.

Equally important is the message that the twenty-first-century highway system must be one that is operated more effectively than that of the twentieth century. Traffic signal timing, incident response, traveler information, and all the other tools available to the traffic engineer must be applied in a manner that ensures that existing roadway capacity is used as efficiently as possible. As discussed in the next chapter, we are not even close to achieving this goal. Given the likelihood of increasing congestion and future funding difficulties, it is essential that we operate the system such that every square inch of pavement is utilized as efficiently as possible.

CHAPTER 6

A Tale of Two Cultures

He who rejects change is the architect of decay.
The only institution that rejects change is the
cemetery.

—Harold Wilson[53]

IMAGINE A GROUP OF ALIEN RESEARCHERS ARRIV-
ing from outer space with the assignment of analyzing the
workings of the U.S. system of state and federal government(s).
Without doubt, the section of their report dealing with the state-
level departments of transportation would conclude that these
departments are in the construction business. In fact, one could
imagine the aliens' confusion over the fact that the departments
have the word transportation in their name, since their primary
focus appears to be on construction and maintenance rather than
facilitating the movement of people and goods throughout the
United States.

The alien researchers might have reached this conclusion
based on their analysis of the publications produced by the state
departments of transportation, including their annual reports.
One sample of this documentation would be the Kansas 2009
annual report, in which the core of Secretary of Transportation
Deb Miller's message is embodied in the following paragraph:

"The most expensive construction project ever led by
KDOT—the $127 million expansion of I-435 in Johnson
County—opened to traffic. The innovative I-35/87th Street

interchange in Lenexa received national recognition. KDOT was honored for maintaining the fifth best state-owned road and highway system in the nation"[54]

The only reference to the fact that KDOT is operating a transportation system and supporting mobility (other than building roads) is indirect, in that it mentions the fact that the department tracks its progress in meeting performance targets in critical areas. There is no mention of the quality of transportation services provided to the citizens and businesses of Kansas in the form of reduced or more reliable travel times, improved safety, changes in congestion, and so on.

But it isn't fair to pick on Kansas. The preceding example is representative of the majority of annual reports produced by transportation agencies, in that they all suffer from the self-image of being in the construction business. This is an understandable bias. Since their creation in the early twentieth century, the mission of the state departments of transportation was the construction of the greatest highway system in the world, and they did a magnificent job. As a result, the skills of their staffs, their personnel policies, their organization, their business systems, and their management structure have all been developed to support the needs of a construction organization.

Once the construction of the highways and bridges has been completed, it is important that they are kept in good repair. But it is equally important that they be utilized as safely and efficiently as possible. The manner in which safe and efficient transportation services are delivered using the existing highway infrastructure is known as management and operations (M&O). M&O is defined as follows:

> Management and operations is the collection of activities and supporting infrastructure (signs, signals, communications, incident management teams, etc.) used to ensure that the available supply of roadway capacity is used as efficiently and effectively as possible. Its objectives are to relieve the impacts of both recurring and non-recurring congestion and to address delays, congestion, safety, air quality, and security. In other words,

M&O encompasses all activities required to ensure smooth safe traffic flow on existing roadways.

To move from the abstract to the specific, consider an arterial roadway with a series of signalized intersections (those of us in the transportation business do not call them stoplights). If the traffic signals successively changed from red to green as you reached each intersection, the traffic along this arterial roadway would flow smoothly and without interruption. Fuel would be consumed efficiently, and vehicle emissions (air pollution) would be minimized. This is an example of good M&O. Conversely, imagine a trip along the same arterial roadway, during which you had to stop at each and every intersection. As you waited at the intersection for the signal to turn from red to green, you observed that no vehicles are present on the cross street. Your delay at the intersection was needless. Frustrating isn't it? This is an example of poor M&O. Good M&O is performed by jurisdictions where signal timing is recalculated (the times at which the signals turn from green to red is adjusted) every three to five years. This activity is performed to account for changes in traffic patterns caused by new development and changes in land use. Unfortunately, 35 percent of the jurisdictions in the United States have never adjusted their timing and fewer than 40 percent adjust the timing every three years.[55] This one example gives you both an appreciation of the extent of poor M&O as well as an indication of the cavalier attitude that many transportation agencies have toward a function that affects all of us

The Tools of Operations

In November 1998, running as a reform party candidate, the professional wrestler Jesse Ventura was elected the thirty-eighth governor of Minnesota. In his attempts to reduce both the size of government and its intrusion into our everyday lives, Ventura sponsored a number of initiatives intended to reduce regulations and restrictions of citizen's activities in the state of Minnesota. From the perspective of the transportation community, one of his best-known actions was his attempt to eliminate an M&O tool known as ramp metering.

If you live in California and many other parts of the country, you are already familiar with ramp metering. It is implemented by installing traffic signals on entrance ramps of freeways. The signals operate differently from a conventional traffic signal in that they rapidly alternate between green and red displays, each of which lasts only a few seconds. There is no yellow display. The objective of ramp metering is to reduce the rate at which vehicles enter the freeway traffic stream on the theory that an excess of vehicle demand causes congestion, which, in turn, reduces the overall throughput of the freeway. If the number of vehicles using the freeway mainline is maintained just below the point at which stop-and-go flow occurs, the freeway will be operating at its peak efficiency, and motorists' travel times and safety will be improved.

However, Ventura viewed ramp metering as a government intrusion into citizen's lives and set out to eliminate the technology from Minnesota's freeways—primarily in the Minneapolis area. The state's engineering professionals objected, indicating that ramp metering was highly beneficial to traffic flow and should be retained. A compromise was negotiated in which the state would evaluate the operation of the freeways and surrounding streets with the ramp metering in operation. The ramp metering would then be turned off, and a second evaluation would be conducted. The two evaluations would then be compared. In this way, the effectiveness (or lack of effectiveness) of the system could be determined. The results were astounding. Travel times without ramp metering were 22 percent higher than they were when ramp metering was operating. Accident rates jumped 25 percent without ramp metering.[56] These results are an indication of the power of a single M&O tool.

As you read these results, the obvious question is: why isn't ramp metering installed on all urban freeways? The answer is instructive. Ramp metering is effective in areas that experience regular congestion—typically inner cities. Traffic in the suburbs (whose residents tend to be more affluent then those of the inner city) is lighter and uncongested. Thus in many areas, ramp metering restricts the lower income residents of an urban area from using the freeway while providing the upper income residents with unrestricted access and improved travel. This is looked upon as an unacceptable subtle form of class discrimination. For this reason, an effective engineering solution to traffic congestion often becomes a political *hot potato*. In general, locations that have successfully implemented ramp metering do not have the well-defined social strata found in many older urban areas.

Ironically, the reverse situation exists on I-270 in the Maryland suburbs of Washington, DC. In this case, the higher income residents live closer to the city in communities such as Bethesda and Chevy Chase while the less affluent residents live in more distant suburbs of Damascus and Germantown. With wealth comes political influence, a factor that discourages the use of ramp metering on I-270. These two examples provide a graphic example of the degree to which politics can influence the actions of public sector transportation agencies. Since these agencies only survive with the support of the governor and the state legislature, they are hesitant to propose unpopular technologies.

M&O tools

Like ramp metering that is used on freeway entrance ramps, every action taken by the owner of an existing roadway to influence the flow of traffic can be considered a form of management and operations. These actions may occur on freeways, arterials, or local roads. They may also include provision of traffic information to motorists about downstream conditions to permit them to divert (if possible) or at least to reduce their frustration. Other items included under the M&O banner are parking management (both charges and availability) and toll collection. M&O strategies might include utilizing electronic technology or dispatching personnel and equipment in response to a temporary interruption of traffic flow such as a crash. Even the GPS navigation devices that you carry in your car to find your way to an unknown destination are considered tools of operations. Road signs and pavement markings may also be considered part of operations. Collectively the operational tools that make use of information technology (IT) have been designated ITS. Some might consider this name to be an oxymoron,

Strategy	Description	Effectiveness
Advanced Vehicle Safety Systems	This is a class of technologies rapidly emerging from the automotive industry that are intended to improve the overall safety of vehicle operations. Examples include back-up warnings, collision warnings, adaptive cruise control, automatic breaking systems, lane departure warnings, etc.	Too varied to apply a single value
Automated Enforcement	Primarily includes speed cameras and red-light running cameras which automate the process of issuing violations to motorists exceeding the speed limit or disobeying traffic signal indications, respectively	Reduced right angle crashes at intersections by as much as 20%
Congestion Pricing	Variously called road pricing and value pricing, this strategy permits motorists to utilize a specific facility or urban area for a fee that varies depending on the levels of congestion that exist at the time that the fee is paid.	Congestion pricing in London's central business district reduced congestion by more than 20%
Electronic Payment Systems	Includes all payments made for use of a roadway, parking or transit facility. These systems provide an automated mechanism (such as EZPass) for rapid collection of fees and fares. This is an enabling technology for congestion pricing and certain parking management systems	Not applicable
Commercial Vehicle Management Systems	Multiple technologies are available to facilitate movement of trucks and buses including weigh in motion (which eliminates the need to stop at truck weigh stations), automated inspection processes, on-line registration, etc.	Too varied to apply a single value
Incident Management	Includes the organization, technology and personnel needed for the rapid identification, response, and removal of vehicle incidents.	Reduced delays during incidents by as much as 50%

TABLE 4a   M&O Strategies

questioning the intelligence of these devices and the accuracy of the information they provide.

This book is not intended to make you an operations expert but rather to acquaint you with the potential of the various operations strategies for relieving congestion, improving safety, and generally improving the quality of travel as an alternative to the construction of new roadways. For this reason, a summary of the available tools is provided in Tables 4a through 4d. More information on the technical details and variations in these strategies can be found in references such as the Handbook of Transportation Systems.[57]

Strategy	Description	Effectiveness
In-Vehicle Navigation	GPS units purchased either as original equipment or after-market devices to provide motorists with the best route from their present location to a desired destination. Newer units include a feature to include real-time travel times in the calculation of shortest route.	Data not available
Lane Control	Most commonly found as displays of green arrows or red X's positioned over individual lanes on freeways and arterials. It is more commonly found in Europe than in the US, where, in addition to being opened and closed, differing speed limits may be posted for individual lanes.	No data available for US lane control systems, although the use of lane controls for shoulders on freeways, and the use of reversible lanes on urban arterials, obviously has the impact to significantly expand capacity of these facilities in the direction that the extra lane is being added. The European approach has the ability to slow traffic on individual freeway lanes also has significant safety benefits.
Parking Management Systems	Parking management systems are used for two strategies: First they may be used to inform drivers about the availability of parking. Second, they may be used to adjust parking rates as a function of time of day to encourage or discourage the use of specific parking facilities or to encourage the use of transit.	No data is available to evaluate the impact of parking management systems, although their obvious benefits are the reduction in traffic that is circulating looking for available parking in congested urban areas. One planning study conducted in Pittsburgh, PA concluded that 1/3 of the traffic within the central business district was circulating looking for parking.
Ramp Metering	Restricts the rate at which vehicles enter a freeway in order to maintain free-flowing traffic on the mainline	Travel times improved 22%, Accidents reduced 25%

TABLE 4b   M&O Strategies-*continued*

Strategy	Description	Effectiveness
Road Weather Information Systems	Road weather information is provided with the intent of improving safety. Systems in use measure visibility, wind, temperature and pavement conditions, and provide information that can be used to alert drivers of potentially unsafe conditions.	No data available
Route Diversion/Corridor Management	Management of traffic flow by influencing motorists' choice of routes is a potentially powerful albeit relatively rare strategy. This strategy is used if a facility is closed due to an incident (crash, construction, weather, etc.). It could also be used (but is not currently) to provide load balancing on parallel facilities, to ensure that all available capacity is utilized to its fullest extent.	Studies have shown that this strategy has the ability to reduce delays by as much as 50% in the event of a long term incident on a major facility, when spare capacity is available on parallel routes.
Traffic Signal Control	The low hanging fruit of the M&O field, improved traffic signal timing offers substantial near term benefits. Additional benefits are possible with more advanced forms of control in which the signal timing is adjusted automatically in response to changing traffic conditions.	Reduced delays by as much as 35%
Traffic Monitoring Systems	Strictly speaking, traffic monitoring is not a stand-alone strategy, but rather it is considered an "enabling technology" that is needed by many other strategies (signal control, ramp metering, route diversion, traveler advisory, etc.). This is the technology that measures traffic flow and travel times on all roadways.	Not applicable since this is not a stand-alone strategy.

TABLE 4c   M&O Strategies-*continued*

Strategy	Description	Effectiveness
Traffic Advisory and Information Systems	This strategy is the collection of techniques used by traffic agencies to communicate with motorists. It includes the sign boards (they are known as variable message signs or dynamic message signs-VMS or DMS), telephone call-in systems, websites, low power highway advisory radio, and connections with the media. One of the most effective traffic advisory systems is the emerging in-vehicle navigation system that comes equipped with the ability to navigate around congested areas.	Some studies have found delay reductions as high as 50%
Variable Speed Limit	For years, traffic engineers have known that the majority of motorists drive at a speed that they consider to be safe under prevailing roadway and traffic conditions. During inclement weather, speeds are often lower than the posted speed limit. During periods of dry pavement, high visibility and light to moderate traffic flows, speeds are often considerably higher than the posted speed limit. With this strategy, variable speed limits would be automatically calculated and posted, so that the regulatory speeds are adjusted to prevailing conditions.	Studies have shown that safety is enhanced when traffic is flowing in a steady unvarying stream, with the great majority of drivers traveling at the same rate.
Work Zone Traffic Management	Work zone traffic management is not a unique strategy, but rather a collection of strategies including traveler advisories, variable speed limits and photo enforcement, all of which are used to regulate the flow of traffic in work zones, in a manner that enhances the safety of the workers and motorists.	Accidents reduced as much as 30%

TABLE 4d M&O Strategies-*continued*

The Power of Operations

While it is unlikely that anyone will read every word of the tables, even a glance at its contents is revealing.

First, you should be impressed by the quantity of M&O strategies available to the roadway operator. If all appropriate strategies were to be implemented, safety would be significantly improved, and delays would be reduced on most of today's roadways. In other words, solutions are available in the form of M&O strategies that could have a significant impact on the quality of travel if they are aggressively and ubiquitously applied.

Second, you should be impressed by the possible magnitude of the improvements. Think about it this way: the reduction of congestion by 25 percent on a three-lane freeway is equivalent to adding an additional lane to that road. Since the cost of new freeway lanes exceed $10 million per mile, it should be obvious that the implementation of a strategy costing a fraction of that amount is very attractive.

Third, you should be impressed by the number of strategies for which there are no available estimates of the benefits. This is a dynamic and changing situation that could be out of date by the time this book is published. However, the current information vacuum is symptomatic of the attitudes of many public agencies that do not understand the importance of reporting progress to their customers—the traveling public. Unless required to report the effectiveness of their investments in new strategies by either the FHWA or a state legislature, agencies rarely bother to measure and/or report the impact of their actions.

So here we have a situation in which a powerful set of M&O tools are available to improve the efficiency of existing highway infrastructure. Yet many of these tools remain unused and unevaluated, in spite of their inherent potential. Moreover, the majority of senior managers employed by transportation agencies are relatively unenthusiastic about their use, possibly because of the absence of hard data regarding their effectiveness, but also because they do not offer the same appeal to the media and public officials as that of opening a new bridge or a new section of highway. In other words, the ribbon-cutting ceremonies that are so popular with politicians don't work for M&O strategies.

If the Strategies of M&O Are So Great, Why Aren't They More Ubiquitous?

The reluctance of the great majority of public agencies to take advantage of available M&O strategies is an additional reason for the failure of the twentieth-century highway system to meet the needs of the twenty-first-century vehicles and their owners. Our inability to establish an aggressive M&O program within transportation organizations can be attributed to three obstacles: (1) the culture of existing transportation agencies, (2) a planning/funding process oriented toward new construction, and (3) fear of new technology (or at least reluctance to take the risks invariably associated with its introduction). These three obstacles are described in this chapter. Eliminating the three obstacles is a more complex process, which is discussed in the concluding section of this book.

The Culture

Assume that you are a developer with a prime piece of property that is in an ideal location for a major new shopping center. You hire an architect to design the new center. The architect's plans are used to request proposals from construction contractors who are interested in developing the center for you. The contractor is selected from among several bidders on the basis of his cost estimate, credentials, and reputation. You are very satisfied with the work performed by the selected contractor. Workmanship is of high quality, and the project is completed within the estimated time and budget. All problems encountered are quickly corrected. Overall, it is a very satisfactory project. And now the time has come to make the transition to the operation of the new shopping center. Retailers must be found to lease the available space, and the public must be encouraged to shop there. The activities associated with the care and feeding of the tenants and their customers are known as operations. These activities might include leasing space, advertising, scheduling special events, installation of plantings and decorations, arranging for janitorial services, law enforcement, and a plethora of other activities. Would you hire the construction contractor to do this work?

Think about it! You have developed a good working relationship with the contractor and his people. His performance has been good, and you feel that he has a competent staff. BUT it is likely that the contractor does not possess the knowledge, skills, and abilities required to perform the required work. He probably cannot offer any prior relationships with potential tenants; he is not familiar with interior design, advertising, or janitorial services. His staff is better suited to carpentry and plumbing rather than dealing with the owner of a dress store. His accounting system is oriented toward the purchase of materials to be used on a construction job rather than sending monthly billings to store owners. In short, he has neither the staff nor the systems associated with the operation of the shopping centers he is so good at constructing.

In general, most transportation agencies are faced with a similar dilemma. The history of the U.S. highway system described in Chapter 1 discusses the creation of the state DOTs during the early twentieth century. You may recall that they were organized with the mission of constructing the nation's highway system. The success of these DOTs was spectacular throughout the twentieth century. The U.S. interstate system is one of their crowning achievements and should probably be considered one of the seven wonders of the world. It has been imitated by many other nations—including most recently China, which is building its own equivalent of the interstate system investing in a 53,000-mile highway system that will rival the existing 47,000-mile U.S. interstate system.

Evidence of the construction orientation that evolved from the activities of the twentieth-century DOTs can be found in the organization charts of most highway agencies. The organization chart of the Rhode Island Department of Transportation (RIDOT), shown in Figure 4 as an example, pays only lip service to M&O, which is organizationally buried three levels down from the office of the director and shown as traffic management and highway safety. Yet the greater importance of the offices of infrastructure development and highway and bridge maintenance (at least in the eyes of the management of RIDOT) is demonstrated by the fact that these two offices are shown one level up from the traffic management and safety activities, reporting directly to the director. The relationships portrayed by the RIDOT organization chart is representative of those found in the majority of state DOTs.

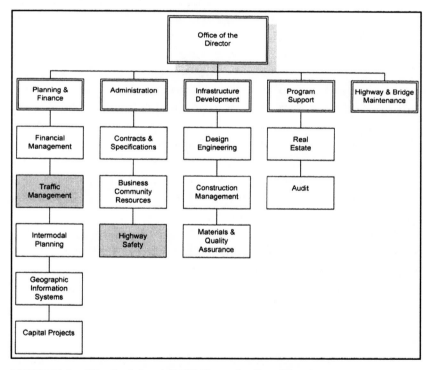

FIGURE 4 Rhode Island DOT Organization Chart

As if organizational issues are not enough, further evidence of the construction culture of transportation agencies can be found by examining the libraries of these same transportation agencies. Most libraries contain construction standards for bridge construction, pavement design, and highway design. They define the manner in which pavement is to be laid, guard rails installed, drainage accommodated, and so on, virtually every activity associated with the construction of a new roadway. It is a rare library that includes statewide standards for ITS designs or communications protocols. When standards exist, they are usually advisory standards or those that have been promulgated by the federal government.

The list goes on. Other incompatibilities between M&O and the construction culture include the salary structures of transportation agencies that are oriented toward civil engineering and construction field personnel rather than more highly paid IT specialists, electrical engineers, and mechanical engineers. State training programs may require new hires to spend time in the field in muddy boots, observing the construction projects that are considered to be the agency's bread and butter. Employees desiring to rise to management position must be registered professional engineers, a designation that reflects the engineer's knowledge of civil engineering technology as opposed to other disciplines such as information technology, telecommunications, and operations research. Construction contracting performed by the transportation agency must be performed on a low-bid basis, whereas contracting for the types of M&O strategies listed in Table 4 requires more complex forms of contracting in which contractor selection is based on the quality of the proposal and the capabilities of the contractor's staff, in addition to cost. Much has been written on this subject, but agencies have been slow to change in spite of the demonstrated benefits and relatively low costs of M&O.

The Project Planning and Funding Process

On September 12, 1962 at Rice University, President John F. Kennedy set a goal for the United States of putting a man on the moon within one decade. His reasons for this goal were clearly defined and included ensuring the peaceful use of outer space and satisfying our quest for scientific knowledge. Although he recognized the technological challenges associated with achieving this goal, his speech did not focus on the development of new technology but rather on advancing the well-being of society.

It's a good thing Kennedy wasn't an engineer. A similar speech given from an engineering perspective would have justified the goal in terms of the development of bigger and better rockets and the opportunity to build more elaborate mission control centers. Engineers would have justified their emphasis of tangible systems on the basis that "politicians only understand things that they can see and touch" and for which ribbon cuttings are possible. This line of reasoning confuses outputs (in highway terms—the lane miles of roadway that have been constructed) with outcomes (again in highway terms—whether we made anyone's travel easier, safer, faster, or more reliable). As far as Kennedy's speech is concerned, there is little doubt that advancing the well-being of society (outcome) is more inspiring than the construction of a more elaborate mission control center (output).

In the world of transportation engineering, I experienced a similar phenomenon that confirmed the public's interest in outcomes rather than outputs. I was recently interviewed by more than a dozen media outlets (radio, TV, and newspapers) in connection with Maryland's Multi Modal Traveler Information System (MMTIS), a cell phone tracking system used to acquire traffic flow data throughout the Baltimore region. In every case, reporters were interested in the outcome—will motorists notice any difference? Not a single reporter asked about the number of cell towers, how the technology worked, or the characteristics of the traffic management center receiving the data.

Yet traditional transportation planning processes emphasize output over outcome, a consideration that works against the integration of M&O strategies into the planning processes. You might ask—who cares? The answer is that we should care a lot since the planning process is the valve that regulates the flow of federal funding to state transportation agencies. Contrary to popular perception, this funding is not just handed over to the states in the form of a single massive grant but arrives with a truckload of regulations and paperwork that must be completed for each and every project. The preparation and federal approval process for this daunting paperwork may take longer than the time required to implement most M&O strategies.

The output/construction bias of the planning process is reflected in one definition of transportation planning that indicates that it "is the field involved with the siting of transportation facilities (generally streets and highways and public transport lines)."[58] Although the federal government has attempted to provide interpretations of the federal aid process that permits planning and funding of M&O activities, the fact remains that in most states and regions, the planning process remains devoted to ensuring an acceptable distribution of funding for the construction of new facilities among all political jurisdictions within an urban area. Until this bias is directly addressed, there will be little hope of achieving the desired balance between construction and M&O.

Because of the many variations in the transportation planning process, it is dangerous to generalize. However, the following three documents are the common denominator of the process.

Long Range Transportation Plan (LRTP): A document resulting from regional or statewide collaboration and consensus on a region or state's transportation system, serving as the defining vision for the region's or state's transportation systems and services. In metropolitan areas, the plan describes all of the transportation improvements scheduled for funding over the next twenty years.

State Transportation Improvement Program (STIP): A staged, multi-year, statewide, multimodal/intermodal program of transportation projects. It is consistent with the statewide transportation plan and planning processes as well as metropolitan plans, TIPs, and processes

Transportation Improvement Program (TIP): A document prepared by a metropolitan planning organization (MPO) that lists projects to be funded for the next one- to three-year period.

These three documents, which receive a high level of attention from planning organizations, are at odds with the concept of M&O for the following reasons:

1. They are used to define projects. M&O is not a project. It does not have a beginning and an end. It is an ongoing,

continuously evolving process. For example, the process of incident management requires a staff of trained personnel equipped with the vehicles and equipment required to respond to crashes and other forms of incidents. Personnel salaries make up the majority of the cost of this activity

2. In fact, capital improvements are only part of M&O, and not the most important part, which is the people, procedures, and protocols used in real time to manage or preempt disruptions.

3. Definition and implementation of construction is a long-term process that reflects the pace of planning, designing, and constructing new facilities (twelve years is the average for a new road). M&O strategies can typically be implemented within two to three years. The time scales of these two categories of activities are obviously incompatible.

4. The planning process is consensus-driven, requiring the agreement of the agencies included in the planning process. Again, the long time frame associated with this process, as well as the need to satisfy all constituent agencies, tends to prevent flexible response to unanticipated needs (such as hurricanes and terrorist attacks), which must be the hallmark of a successful operational program. The consensus-driven program requires participants to anticipate every possible set of circumstances that might be addressed by an operational organization so that consensus can be developed regarding the acceptable response.

While the LRTP, STIP, and TIP are not the only products of planning organizations, they clearly bias the entire spectrum of activities conducted by these organizations, including the tools they use, the brochures and reports they develop, and their interaction with other agencies. For example, I was recently given the opportunity to offer comments on the LRTP being developed for the Baltimore Metropolitan Area.[59] It was clear that this document was no more than a compendium of prioritized construction projects submitted by each of the participating jurisdictions. I suggested that some operational projects be considered, such as regional signal timing or expanded incident response. The suggestion was rejected out of hand because of the danger that it would divert funds from the projects that had been submitted and reduce the number of ribbon-cutting opportunities that might occur with the limited available funding. The two lessons learned (neither of which were a surprise) were that M&O does not fit into this capital budgeting-oriented process and that there are no advocates for regional operations in a bottoms-up planning process designed to address the political desires of politicians from single jurisdictions.

The tools of transportation planning, by which new projects are identified, evaluated, and prioritized, emphasize the construction of facilities that will ease recurring congestion. Yet more than one-half of the delays occurring in the transportation system are due to non-recurring congestion caused by both predicted (sporting events, hurricanes, etc.) and unpredicted events (crashes, terrorist attacks, earthquakes, etc.). Many of the M&O strategies described earlier are specifically developed to address the non-recurring events. Yet planners do not even possess the tools to estimate their benefits.

From the perspective of M&O, the planning process can be considered broken. Neither the process itself nor its supporting tools are capable of ensuring that M&O is at the *funding table*. Yet the twentieth-century highway system will never move to the twenty-first century until the old construction-oriented, bottoms-up planning process, intended to give every jurisdiction a fair piece of the pie, is fixed.

Fear of New Technology

Many years ago, as a transportation systems consultant, I was involved in projects requiring the analysis of aging traffic signal systems to determine if they should be replaced, either because of degraded reliability or inadequate functionality.

These studies addressed many aspects of the signal system reliability and effectiveness, but the primary question to be answered was whether or not these systems had reached the end of their useful lives. Answering this question required a review of maintenance records to determine whether the equipment failure rate and its associated maintenance cost per intersection had increased to the point at which their ongoing maintenance costs exceeded the cost of replacement with a new system. These studies required a review of the jurisdiction's signal maintenance records, which invariably existed in the form of a disorganized stack of handwritten faded time sheets instead of computerized maintenance data that could be used to facilitate a study of this nature. Now, nearly thirty years later, PCs and user-friendly software are ubiquitous. Yet, according to a recent survey, only 10 percent of agencies with signal system maintenance responsibilities have implemented computerized maintenance records systems (which could be as simple as an Excel spreadsheet). In other words, this straightforward technology with its obvious benefits is not being used even though it has been available for decades.

Is this simple example representative of the pace of technology adoption by the public sector? If so, does it matter? If it does matter, how can we cure the problem? These significant questions cannot be ignored if the United States transportation system is to effectively address rapidly growing travel demand and stagnant funding.

In an effort to determine whether the preceding example is symptomatic of the public sector's reluctance to adopt new technologies, a sample of technologies related to M&O, infrastructure, toll collection, automotive telematics,[60] and consumer products was reviewed. The results of this review are shown in Table 5 and plotted in Figure 5. The horizontal axis of the figure approximates the degree to which organizations using technology-based products are connected to their customers, or in other words, whether they are public or private sector organizations.

Technology	Category	Years to Adoption	Comments
Traffic signal systems that automatically adjust to traffic demand	ITS	20+	Modern traffic control systems known as SCOOT (from England) and SCATS (from Australia) were introduced during the 1980s.
Ramp Metering	ITS	40+	1963 Eisenhower Freeway in Chicago Today, 16% of freeway ramps are metered
Traffic Monitoring	ITS	30+	Vehicle detectors introduced in the 1960s Currently installed on less than 50% of urban freeways and 6% of urban arterials
Fiber Reinforced Polymers (FRPs)	Materials	30+	In existence since the 1940s. Still not used to any significant extent for bridge decks
Shoulder Rumble Strips	Pavement	15	Initial installations prior to 1988 Still being studied by some DOTs
EZPass Electronic Toll Collection Systems	Electronic Payment	5	Implemented by TBTA in 1995 Installed by PANY in 1997 Available since 1990 according to Mark IV
Navigation Systems	Vehicle Telematics	7+	First system in 1983 and introduced in 1990 First GPS-based vehicle navigation system introduced by Magellan in 1995. By 1996 40 total sales exceeded 1 mill. units
Web Browser Technology	Consumer & Business Products	1	Time to 10 million users

TABLE 5   Adoption of New Technology

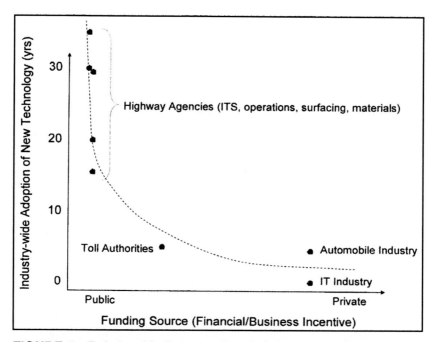

FIGURE 5 Relationship Between Funding Sources and Adoption of New Technology

The results are not encouraging for those who are anxious to see the twentieth-century highway system evolve into a more advanced system of the twenty-first century. They paint a collective picture of a public sector transportation community that continues its use of older entrenched technologies and practices without concern for the potential benefits of new and useful developments.

While these exhibits are not based on a carefully conducted scientific survey, there can be little doubt that the information presented is representative of the technology adoption timeframes for each of the business sectors presented. Admittedly, it would be easy to argue with these results since there are numerous definitional issues regarding the time when a technology becomes available and the number of agencies, manufacturers, and/or customers that constitute its acceptance. In spite of these limitations, it is clear that the auto industry with its recent emphasis on reduced product cycles and the IT industry with its rush to market are more proactive in their technology adoption strategies than the majority of public transportation agencies. In other words, industries that derive their income directly from the expenditures of their customers (and by implication customer satisfaction) are more agile than their publicly funded counterparts.

It is unacceptable for travelers and shippers to wait more than thirty years for the public sector transportation industry to adopt potentially beneficial technological advances. Yet it would also be unfair and inaccurate to conclude that these problems are caused by uncaring public employees. In fact the majority of problems that can be identified are associated with the environment in which a public agency operates, including:

- Public sector transportation industry is large and diverse. While there are approximately a dozen automobile manufacturers producing a relatively homogenous product, the public sector transportation industry is represented by hundreds (if not thousands) of organizations ranging from very large state DOTs to agencies in small towns employing a part-time traffic engineer. It would be unreasonable to expect this broad range of agencies to adopt new technology at the same pace.
- Employees receive few, if any, rewards for the successful development or adoption of new technology and are likely to be penalized for failure. For public employees, the *safe approach* is to avoid change.
- Elected officials and the media evaluate the effectiveness of transportation agencies based on projects completed and funds expended rather than measures that are important to travelers—travel time, travel reliability, travel cost, etc.
- The public sector procurement system, which emphasizes competitive selection of systems and services, discourages the use of proprietary new technologies offered by a single provider.

- The procurement process favors the low-bid selection of offerers. It rarely accounts for the best technical solution, life-cycle costs, and overall effectiveness.
- The customer provides the funding for private sector products and services—that is, an automobile purchaser is both the customer and the funding source. The public sector's income is primarily tax based. The distribution of public funding is never based on past performance and may be more related to political influence and considerations of fairness than the needs of its customers (travelers and shippers)

These structural deficiencies must be corrected before the public sector can be expected to creatively and aggressively adopt new technology for improved service delivery. If this does not occur, the gap between the state-of-the-art and the state-of-the-practice within the public sector will continue to grow to the detriment of travelers as well as the nation's economy.

The Picture is Not Completely Bleak

This chapter paints a grim picture of conservative public transportation agencies with a construction culture that are poorly equipped to manage the transition to the twenty-first century. Although there are numerous problems, there are glimmers of hope. Many departments of transportation are operating incident management programs that emphasize rapid response and removal of crashes on interstate roadways. In addition, many departments are providing improved traveler information through websites, telephone messages received by dialing 511, and posting travel times on variable message signs. The federal government is placing increased emphasis on operations through a combination of research, training, and regulation. It is likely that the next highway bill passed by congress will require states to implement a performance measurement program through which they can assess their progress toward providing improved transportation services.

However, we've got a long way to go and many obstacles to overcome. Efforts to date have been overly cautious and have emphasized interstate travel, ignoring the remaining 50 percent of travel that occurs on other roadways. The daunting combined challenges of funding shortages, the construction culture, the crippled planning process, and technological inertia must be addressed if further progress is to be made.

CHAPTER 7

The Many Faces of Customer Service

It is not enough to give customers excellent service. You must subtly make them aware of the great service they are getting.

—Unattributed Quote[61]

~~~~~~

IN THEORY, TRANSPORTATION AGENCIES CANNOT expect the public acceptance (and funding) needed to support their mission unless their customers and elected officials appreciate the service they are providing. However, this is not completely true. It is ironic that within the public sector transportation community, funding received by these agencies is in inverse proportion to the quality of the service provided. In other words, as it becomes more difficult to travel on the nation's highways (poor service), elected officials are increasingly willing to increase the funding provided for transportation improvements (more money). Even more ironic is the fact that catastrophes produce funding windfalls for those agencies involved in the catastrophe. Talk about a perverted system!

If you doubt the accuracy of these statements, think about the bridge collapse on I-35W in Minnesota. In August 2007, the eight-lane interstate bridge over the Mississippi River collapsed, killing 13 people and injuring 135. The collapse of a major interstate bridge is an extremely rare occurrence. In this unfortunate case, transportation services in the Minneapolis area were disrupted for more than a year, costing travelers who had been using the bridge an estimated $400,000 per day in lost revenue and delays. Adding the $234 million cost of the new bridge, the total cost of the collapse to the traveling and taxpaying public was more than $300 million. However, as a result of this catastrophe, the Minnesota Department of Transportation (Mn/DOT) received $250 million in emergency funding from the Federal Emergency Disaster Relief program for the replacement bridge, a structure that has been named project of the year by the American Public Works Association for its design and incredibly rapid construction. In other words, catastrophe breeds success.

This is not a unique example. Consider for example, a recent catastrophe in Montgomery County, Maryland in which the county's twenty-year-old traffic signal computer failed, with disastrous results. Without the computer, the county's population of nearly one million was faced with long backups and greatly increased travel time that resulted from the county's poor backup signal timing. The fact that this system had been designed without adequate provision for operation without the traffic control computer was ignored by the media. Emphasis was placed on the fact that the system was old and underfunded. As a result, the county's department of public works is assured of receiving money for a replacement system. If this problem had not occurred, near-term funding for the new system would have been uncertain at best.

There are many other examples, including the blizzard of Valentine's Day 2007 that stranded motorists on Pennsylvania's roads for nearly a day. The poor response to this storm led to improvements in Pennsylvania DOT's (PennDOT's) emergency response and communications systems. And the list goes on, featuring the impacts of natural disasters such as earthquakes and hurricanes, major accidents, infrastructure failures such as bridge collapses, and so on. The natural conclusion is that if an agency needs more funding, it should pray for a catastrophe. What a way to run a railroad!

So why should the customers (the traveling public) be made aware of the great service they are getting (assuming the service can be considered great)? And why should anyone worry about their goodwill?

In addition to the obvious fact that the vast majority of DOT employees joined the public sector with a genuine desire to improve society, there are many reasons that public transportation agencies and their employees should be focused on the provision of good customer service. First, not all public sector jobs are equally secure. For example, at the state level, the secretaries of transportation as well as their deputies are typically political appointees who serve at the will of the governor.

Customer service should also receive a high priority within public sector transportation agencies because the survival of the agency in its present form depends on the public's satisfaction with its performance. Many agencies have increasingly turned to outsourcing of agency functions to the private sector either because of the political benefits of being able to claim that the public workforce has been reduced or because of an impression, whether true or not, that the private sector can perform the same job more effectively. Good customer service is essential if agency personnel want to reduce the possibility of increased outsourcing.

Performance measurement (how well are we doing), which can be considered a component of customer service, is receiving increased attention within the transportation community. Performance is measured for a number of important reasons, not the least of which is communicating with the public and elected officials regarding the quality of services provided. Effective performance measurement should also include benchmarks that describe how well the situation will improve in the future and how well it has already been improved as a result of the agency's efforts. In some cases, performance measures can be used to compare performance measures with those of other agencies in order to brag about the outstanding job being done or to justify the need for additional funding (the perverted logic again). For this reason, increased emphasis on performance measurement can be used to support outreach to the customers of the various transportation departments.

Public-Private Comparisons

It is a popular theory that the public sector is concerned with the public good while the private sector is only interested in financial profit. This comparison is frequently offered as the basis for the continuing existence of organizations responsible for the management of the highway system as public agencies, rather than assigning responsibility for surface transportation to a franchised utility or a private sector company. But is this true? If one were to conduct a survey that examines the public's view of the orientation of the two sectors, the results would be very different. Generally, the public sector is viewed as being difficult to deal with because of its monopolistic hold on the services it provides. The private sector is viewed as being more responsive to their customer's needs because of the competitive environment in which it operates. Thus, while public sector employees, including those in the transportation sector, may have the best of intentions, the face they show to their customers is generally one of dispassionate indifference.

Comparisons of the airline industry (private sector) with the highway transportation industry (public sector) demonstrate this difference. Statistics are regularly produced by and for the industry that include the percent of on-time arrivals and percentage of lost baggage for all origins and destinations and flights. This information is used by many travelers as a consideration in the selection of airlines and flights. How many departments of transportation publish equivalent information for highway travelers—travel times and travel time reliability statistics for all roadways and all times of day? How many agencies are willing to make the investment required to provide information at this level of detail? The airline industry is presenting a customer service-oriented face to the public while the highway industry is presenting one of indifference. Obviously, not all private sector companies are created equal, just as not all transportation agencies are created equal. However, there is much to be learned from the good and bad in both sectors. But it is universally true that a private sector company in a competitive environment will rarely survive if it provides poor customer service.

Customer service is not an activity that can be assigned to a single organizational entity within a department of transportation. It is a state of mind that must permeate the organization.

It must be included in every project, publication, and service offered by the organization. Many of the opportunities for customer service can be captured with little additional cost to the agency.

Annual reports reflect the customer service orientation: Medtronic is a company that produces medical equipment used to "treat disorders such as heart disease, spinal conditions, neurological disorders, vascular disease, and diabetes."[62] The culture of customer service permeates the Medtronic organization, including its publications, call centers, and website as well as the actions of its employees.

Medtronic is a publicly held company whose performance is evaluated by its shareholders based on its financial success. But its customers (as opposed to the shareholders) think of it as a company whose performance and products directly affect their quality of life. Shouldn't this also be true of highway transportation agencies? The examples presented here portray a philosophy that exists throughout the Medtronic organization. They demonstrate the philosophy that customer service is not the responsibility of a single department but one that must be continuously applied through the actions of all employees at all times.

When reading the following examples, note the emphasis on *you* the customer rather than *we* the organization. In other words, Medtronic is concerned about *you* and not about *we* (ourselves). Also note the relative number of times that *you* and *we* are used in the public sector examples.

The Medtronic annual report is focused on its customers. The company describes its products in terms of the manner in which it has improved their lives. There are no technical descriptions of products, only discussions of people. In other words, the company speaks of *you* as opposed to *we*. The cover of the Medtronic annual report has a photograph of a patient wearing a Medtronic tee shirt. The photographs of the company's CEO and president show them on a soccer field with a smiling young boy, a customer of the Medtronic insulin delivery system, holding a soccer ball. The caption over the picture states that:

Medtronic CEO Art Collins and President Bill Hawkins
(WE) met recently with 8-year old Raphael Lang (YOU)
who has diabetes. His (YOU) MiniMed Paradigm
REAL-Time System, an insulin pump capable of dis-
playing real-time glucose data, gives him (YOU) greater
control in managing glucose levels compared to insulin
injections. So now Raphael (YOU) has more flexibility
to play his favorite sports when he (YOU) wants.

YOU and WE have been added to the quote to emphasize the
orientation of this caption toward the customer.

Contrast this approach with the reports of most DOTs.
Rather than speaking of the customer, their annual reports are
internally focused. They contain narratives of successful construction projects, as well as the size and extent of their agency's
responsibilities. The authors of some annual reports seem to feel
that the public would appreciate their efforts if they just got to
know their employees. As a result, they portray their employees' job responsibilities along with any awards they might have
received. Not a word about the customer. These annual reports
rarely mention customer service in terms of improved quality of life from the perspective of the transportation system
performance.

For example, the first page of one state's annual report
begins with the following highlighted message about *we* from
the chairman of the state transportation commission:

Not too many people know this, but we are also responsible for all traffic safety programs, such as anti-DWI
campaigns, seat belt use education, and child seat
restraint use projects. Our seat belt use has climbed over
90 percent this year, and our campaign to stem drunken
driving is also paying off with the number of alcohol-
involved crashes down from this time last year.[63]

This statement has been quoted in total. While the results
are admirable, there are no other introductory or concluding
sentences that describe the agency's business and its concern

with the needs of its customers. This report and most others like it, include posed photographs of the secretary of transportation as well as the transportation commission chairman. It also includes pictures of employees at work, awards ceremonies, and construction projects. In fairness, the annual report used for this example also includes statistics related to environment, safety, and infrastructure condition. However, it fails to provide the needed emphasis on customer service, in spite of the fact that "Operate as a Customer Focused Organization" is identified as one of the goals of the DOT used in this example.

Websites Reflect a Similar Bias

The Medtronic website homepage includes a number of different navigation tabs including: patients (titled "Your Health"), physicians, employment, and information about the company. When navigating to the tab for patients, the user is greeted with the heading: Discover More—Wellness starts with understanding. The second level of this page offers several selections the first of which is "Patient Services: Call, write, email, or fax us. We're here for you."[64] Note the use of the *you* versus *we* wording.

Contrast this approach with the website of one state department of transportation that begins with the following paragraph:

> We answer many of the same questions repeatedly. To get an immediate answer to a question that may have been asked by someone else, please try submitting items to our Frequently Asked Question Search below or search our site using the Search XXX GO Button above.[65]

The difference between the cultures and philosophies of these two websites and the organizations they represent is obvious. Is it any wonder that the public does not view the public sector agencies as organizations concerned with provision of high-quality services to their customers?

Websites are powerful tools for customer service and should be used as a mechanism for conveying the agency's customer service orientation. One good example is Rhode Island's website, which contains the heading "Your Concern is Our Concern." Note the use of the *you* versus *we* philosophy. The website begins with the statement that "As part of our renewed commitment to public service, the Rhode Island Department of Transportation (RIDOT) has established a Customer Service Office. The purpose of the Customer Service Office is to keep information lines open between the citizens of Rhode Island (YOU) and RIDOT (WE)."[66] (Here again, the YOU and WE have been added to the quote.)

Many states and some cities have effectively used the Internet to enhance communications with their customers. The Washington, DC local government has established an easy to use website that also begins with a heading that follows the *you* versus *we* principle. This website begins with the heading "How may we help you?"[67] It offers five forms of communication between the government and its citizens including:

- Talk to the Mayor—who will respond personally to an emailed suggestion or observation
- Service Request—the mechanism by which citizens can either request a service or track a prior request
- How's our service—a questionnaire that allows citizens to share their opinion of the services received
- Feedback—ways in which DC services can be improved
- Webmaster—ways in which improvements to the website can be submitted.

Clearly the most successful websites are the ones that reflect this type of customer service orientation. It is also refreshing to be able to cite a number of good examples related to the transportation community. Things might be improving.

Customer Service is Embodied by Accessibility

As consumers we know that nothing can be more frustrating than an attempt to find the *right person* within a large organization. Several years ago, I was involved with a highly publicized effort to re-time the traffic signals in the Washington, DC region.

As a result of an article in the *Washington Post* that identified my association with the effort, I received a number of telephone calls. The common theme of these calls was "who do I speak with about signal timing issues?" Callers were frustrated, and in some cases irate, at their inability to find the appropriate person with whom to discuss traffic signal operation.

Medtronic customers do not experience this frustration. Telephone numbers are available on the company's website, and customers are in frequent contact with the appropriate representatives who assist them with all types of problems from questions about equipment operation to replacement of faulty components to assistance with insurance claims. Following interactions with a company representative, a customer will receive an email such as the one titled "Customer service experience with Medtronic."

> Thank you for contacting Medtronic Diabetes earlier this week. In an effort to continue improving our services, we would appreciate your participation in a quick 5-minute survey reflecting your recent service experience.

Whether answered or not, the fact that the questionnaire was sent is a message that the organization is concerned with its quality of service.

With some exceptions, few transportation agencies operate call centers that are continuously staffed. A well-run call center should be open twenty-four hours a day, seven days a week, reflecting the continuous operation of the transportation system. Call center staff should be required to log all calls and should be empowered to respond to callers' requests and questions. Most important, call center operators should be required to follow up on all calls to ensure that callers' requests have been satisfied. Imagine the reaction of a caller requesting a pothole repair who receives a call back indicating the date for which the repair was scheduled and another call back following that date to ensure that the work was performed satisfactorily. These steps represent high quality customer service and cost very little to implement.

The cost of this level of service need not be excessive. Many DOTs operate traffic operations centers (TOCs) that are staffed continuously with individuals who could provide call center services. These centers experience periods of intense activity followed by periods of inactivity. Similar resources such as administrative personnel may exist in other parts of an organization to provide the call center services. The key to successful operation is adequate training, empowerment, and processes to ensure that calls are answered properly and adequate follow up is provided. To do otherwise is an indication of inadequate concern about customer service. TOC managers tell me that they are concerned about assuming call center responsibility for their agency since they are swamped with calls during major incidents. Utilities and others in similar situations address this problem using pre-recorded messages indicating that they are already aware of the situation and asking the caller to leave a message or respond to an automated system if they have additional concerns. The recorded message also provides additional information regarding the status of the major incident that might be the subject of the call.

One successful demonstration of the principles described here is a call center introduced by VDOT in 2010. Citizens need only to call 1-800-FOR-ROADS to report any problems they see on the highway, to ask questions about construction projects, or generally to communicate anything on their mind about the transportation system. The service is heavily advertised and offers the potential for a significant improvement in VDOT's customer service. The VDOT service is not unique. It is encouraging that an increasing number of agencies are addressing their customer service shortcomings.

Performance Measures and Customer Service

Transportation aficionados might find the inclusion of performance measurement in a chapter titled customer service as a curious juxtaposition of the two subjects. After all, performance measures are collected and used for many different reasons, including justification of new projects to elected officials, evaluation of staff performance, identification of the need for improvements in agency operation, and so on. The dissemination of performance information is a key element of customer service. How can customers be aware of the fact that they are receiving excellent service if no one evaluates and publicizes the service? Alternatively, how do citizens and elected officials know that they are receiving a reasonable return on their investment of tax dollars in the agencies they support?

Gainesville Regional Utilities (GRU), owned by the city of Gainesville, Florida, is the fifth-largest municipal electric utility in the state of Florida. A visit to their website reveals that they "work hard to provide electric reliability that is above the national average." The national statistics are explained in the following manner:

> The ASAI (average service availability index) determines the total time, expressed as a percentage, that electric power is available on demand to customers. The national average for outages including all interruptions was 99.96, and the national average excluding major storms was 99.98. Our percentages are normally above the national average, which means GRU provides reliable electricity service and responds quickly to calls regarding power outages.[68]

This is an example of a public sector agency utilizing national performance measures to establish goals for their operation. The website adds credibility to this statement through an explanation of the manner in which citizens should report power outages, including an automated system that permits customers to pre-register so that their reporting of power outages is automatically sent to a dispatcher without the need to enter any additional information.

This example is in stark comparison with the performance measurement that occurs in the transportation community. First, the transportation community does not maintain national statistics comparable to the national average of power outages, even though similar measures such as roadway closures exist. Various agencies may collect this type of data sporadically, but none of them adhere to a single standard definition of travel interruption. In fact, a phobia exists within the transportation community against any sort of comparisons with either national statistics or with each other.

Second, it is significant that GRU used the national statistics to establish performance goals for themselves. They did not shy away from the possibility that Gainesville might be at a disadvantage because it is subject to an unusually high number of thunderstorms during the summer or that it might be at a disadvantage because of the heavy tree canopy with the potential for dropping branches on power lines. After all, Gainesville has been named Tree City USA by the National Arbor Day Foundation every year since 1982. These are the types of reasons employed by the transportation community to avoid comparisons of their performance with anyone else. Their excuses are that they have unusually heavy traffic, their roads are more winding and hilly, or their weather is worse.

Third, it is significant that GRU has a plan to minimize their power interruptions. They are proud of their exceptional service, they advertise their results, and they are collaborating with their customers to ensure its continued improvement. They are subtly reminding their customers about the great service they are receiving. Contrast this approach with that of the Potomac Electric Power Company (PEPCO) of Maryland, whose service statistics are well below the national average. As a result, local elected officials constantly have PEPCO management on the run, defending their actions and promising major financial commitments to upgrade their service.

Collaboration is not to be overlooked as a customer service technique since it offers the dual benefits of improving the agency's image while enhancing its performance. One compelling example can be found in the way that some agencies interact with callers complaining about a traffic signal operation issue. The call may be as simple as a burned out bulb or a more complex problem such as the traffic signal seems to be stuck. When a more complex problem is received, the individual answering the phone takes the time to explain the operation of the intersection to the caller. The trouble report is then checked. Whether or not the problem was legitimate, a return call is made to the caller who is thanked for the call and who then receives a brief description of the disposition of the repair. The intersection is then reviewed with the caller, and the agency employee asks whether the caller would be willing to keep an eye on the intersection in the future. The caller is now an educated individual who is providing a free and valuable service to the agency. In other words, a caller who intended to complain is now a collaborator with the agency. Everyone wins. The agency has another pair of eyes keeping track of its equipment. The agency also has an advocate for its operation.

From the perspective of performance measurement, the agency's signal failure statistics would be improved, since problems are identified more quickly and accurately by a group of informed citizens, and false calls are reduced. In this way, performance measurement and customer service are inextricably linked.

The Trick is Instituting a Customer Service Culture

Many of the principles of customer service described here were developed by the profit-oriented private sector in their attempts to ensure that their hard-won customers are completely satisfied and will remain customers in the future.

If they are to remain in their current form, transportation agencies will have to study the ways in which the private sector delivers customer service. It will not be acceptable in the future to whine about the lack of respect received from citizens and elected officials. The lack of respect is due to customer service shortcomings. Travelers are quick to recognize that many public transportation agencies consider them a necessary inconvenience rather than customers of those responsible for the management of the nation's transportation system.

There are many ways in which a creative organization can improve its customer service through such simple actions as:

- Bumper stickers on agency vehicles that provide a phone number if unsafe or discourteous operation is observed.
- Fixed signs on variable message signs (VMS) that provide a phone number for motorists to call if incorrect information is being displayed.

- Improved listings in public telephone directories that simplify a customer's ability to navigate the bureaucratic maze
- Require the customer service orientation of all employees, possibly including recognition of employees who have provided exemplary customer service

Most important is the development of a culture that continuously focuses on the subject of customer service. This is a culture that is sensitive to the application of *you* versus *we*. It is a culture that examines the impact of all its activities and products on customer service. Models such as Medtronic should be studied and contrasted with existing agency products and performance. If this does not occur, the privatization of public agencies may be a long-term possibility.

In many respects, the slow emergence of customer service as a priority of public transportation agencies is the result of their construction culture. When building new roads, a well-defined set of procedures must be followed to interact with citizens who are being adversely affected by the construction. This is typically an adversarial relationship that is not compatible with good relations with the users of the highway system. The transition from construction to M&O represents a significant change to this relationship. Customer service must become a high priority if today's public agencies are going to survive in their present form in order to participate in the creation of the twenty-first-century highway system.

Part II
Moving Into the Twenty-First Century

What does it take to turn today's twentieth-century roads and their supporting institutions into a twenty-first-century success?

CHAPTER 8

The Twenty-First Century—A Glimpse of the Possibilities

*For tomorrow belongs to the people who
prepare for it today.*

—African Proverb[69]

~~~~~~

UNTIL NOW, WE HAVE FOCUSED ON DESCRIBING THE
current state of that valuable asset known as the U.S. highway
system. We have discussed its increasing congestion and safety
issues, as well as the problems associated with the institutions that are responsible for its operation. The discussion of
each facet of the system ended with the conclusion that we are
describing a twentieth-century system and not a twenty-first-
century system. By now, you should be asking yourself, what
is a twenty-first-century system anyway? This chapter contains
several visions of the future that might be used to define the
characteristics of this twenty-first-century system. So let's have
some fun.

A Vision for the Near Future

Life as a single father in 2016 (only five years into the
future) can be stressful. Jon Swift pushed his kids out the door,
gulped down a cup of coffee, and left for work. Jumping into his
hybrid sedan, Jon pressed his thumb against the dashboard for
recognition by its biosensor system, which enabled him to start
the engine and activate the vehicle's electronics systems. As he

backed out of his driveway, Jon used the car's voice recognition system to ask his ISP (information service provider) for the best route to work. Jon's on-time arrival at work was particularly critical today because of an important early meeting he was to attend. Jon might have logged onto the Internet to request the status of the transportation system before leaving home. But his hectic morning schedule prevented him from planning his commute until his trip had begun. He might even have used his personal digital assistant (PDA) to receive Internet information from his car, but Jon, like most commuters, preferred the fully integrated voice-activated features of the onboard system.

The synthesized voice of the onboard system responded to Jon's query, asking him if he was traveling to his usual morning destination. Jon answered with a brief "yes," to which the system responded with the bad news that that there was an incident on his favorite route. He was then offered two alternatives, each of which was accompanied by an estimated cost and travel time. The first alternative was a different route, and the second alternative was mass transit. As a resident of the Washington, DC region, Jon was fortunate to have rail mass transit readily available, even though the service tended to be crowded and unreliable. Rail service reliability and status as well as parking availability were taken into consideration by the ISP's recommendation of mass transit as an alternative. Jon swore under his breath at this news since even the shortest route meant that he would arrive at work late. It seemed to him that regional travel continued to deteriorate in spite of the sophisticated new systems that were now in use, but he was grateful that his unexpected delays were modest. He wondered what his life would be like without his ISP and the regional mass transportation systems.

Incidents such as the one that ruined Jon's morning had become increasingly rare as newer vehicles entered the fleet equipped with collision warning systems. As the telematics of twenty-first-century vehicles became increasingly sophisticated, including features such as collision and lane departure warnings, crashes due to driver inattention had decreased significantly. However, older vehicles without such equipment remained in the fleet with the result that crashes had not yet become a thing of the past. In addition, an increased number of elderly drivers with their slower reaction times continued to challenge transportation safety experts as well as the designers of the in-vehicle telematics.

Meanwhile, behind the scenes and unknown to Jon Swift, several organizations were working to facilitate his travel. Because of the growth in regional travel demand and the continuing failure of the region to add transportation capacity, Jon's commute would have been much worse had it not been for the efforts of these organizations:

The National Traveler Information Service (NTIS): a public/ private partnership that had been established in a similar fashion to the National Weather Service to collect traffic data on all of the roadways included in the national highway system. This service used a variety of techniques to collect its traffic data from a variety of commercial and government sources. The NTIS was considered to be a wholesaler of traveler information since it did not directly distribute this information to end-users.

The state department of transportation: an agency with operations responsibilities very similar to the DOTs of the twentieth century but with greatly expanded capabilities. The incident that delayed Jon Swift's commute had been reported to the state police by a motorist's cell phone call to 911. The police had then forwarded this information to the DOT and the NTIS, along with an estimate of the likely duration of the incident and its impact on travel times. The DOT activated its decision support software to project the impact of the incident and to identify the optimum set of actions required to reduce its effect on travelers. On the day of Jon's travel, the recommended actions included the coordinated closure of freeway ramps, signal retiming, and public dissemination of diversion information in order to balance the traffic loads on parallel facilities. If the incident had been more severe, neighboring states would have been asked to provide assistance through additional diversion of long-distance traffic away from the impacted corridor.

The information service provider (ISP): a commercial service that acted as a retailer of the wholesale information furnished by the NTIS. The ISP's revenue was derived from motorists like Jon who relied on a reliable source of transportation system status information. Various ISPs offered differing types of service for automobile, commercial vehicle, and transit travelers.

The preceding story was written in 2006, more than four years prior to the preparation of this book. Since that time, ISPs of the type described here have emerged as viable commercial enterprises. You know these ISPs. They have names like Apple, Google, Garmin, TomTom, and Blackberry. The NTIS has also emerged in the form of private firms such as INRIX and Traffic.com instead of the public sector agency that was envisioned. In addition, safety-related features of in-vehicle telematics are offered on some of the upscale vehicles with the prospects for migration to lower-end products in the future. Four years is an extremely short period of time. Yet the projected advances occurred in less than half the time that was predicted in this story prepared in 2006. Twenty-first-century vehicles are becoming pretty exciting. Imagine what the next four years will bring.

On the other hand, traffic operations personnel will consider the role played by the state DOT as science fiction. Few advances of the type predicted by this story have been made. At the time of this publication, no agency has developed plans for proactive diversion of traffic in the event of a major incident. So this small example demonstrates how the private sector with its twenty-first-century vehicles is aggressively pursuing the promise of the twenty-first century while the public sector remains mired in the culture of the twentieth century. The twenty-first-century highway could look like the description above in which traffic is automatically diverted to parallel facilities and the available highway capacity is used to the fullest extent.

Implicit in the science fiction of the state DOT are a number of technologies that are available today but rarely implemented. These include:

- Coordinated operation of freeways and adjacent urban arterials on which traffic loads are balanced and shifted through a combination of incentives and disincentives to the use of these facilities. Ultimately it might be possible to automate these functions.

- Implementation of a suite of adaptive strategies in which signal timing, ramp metering rates, ramp closures, variable message sign displays, and highway advisory radio broadcasts are continuously adjusted and their impacts evaluated until the desired response (throughput, load balancing, diversion, speed change, etc.) is achieved
- Adaptive value pricing (congestion pricing, road pricing, etc.) in which user costs are adjusted in real-time until desired demand levels are achieved
- Coordination of transit schedules and routes with traffic conditions, such that additional transit capacity is provided on routes experiencing unusual congestion during incident conditions
- Development and application of sophisticated prediction techniques that can be communicated to motorists for near-term trip planning and for prepositioning of incident response resources
- Routine use of decision support tools that permit system operators to evaluate the consequences of various combination of actions in order to ensure effective response to unusual conditions

This list is not necessarily complete but is offered to demonstrate that the beginnings of the twenty-first-century highway system are within our reach.

A Vision for the More Distant Future

Predicting a more distant future can be a risky business. Yet undaunted by the perils of such predictions, a more distant future is forecast based on the certainty that demand is likely to continue to increase while increases in available capacity will be modest at best. This would imply the need for a reservation system similar to the system used by most other forms of transportation: airlines, trains, and ships. The alternative to a reservation system such as the one described here is a congestion pricing system in which the cost of driving in congested areas is significant. This is a choice that must be made by society. However, the following anecdote describes one possible future vision for the mid-twenty-first century.

Two thousand and eight was a significant year. For the first time in history, half of the world's exploding population lived in urban areas. It is expected that the growth of urban areas will continue such that by 2030, 60 percent of the world's population—4.9 billion people—will live and work in urban areas. It is also anticipated that by 2020, there will be twenty-two megacities (urban areas with populations exceeding 10 million) with a combined gross domestic product (GDP) of approximately $4.9 trillion.[70] As transportation specialists, our challenge is to ensure that the quality of life in these urban areas is preserved through the creation and operation of an environmentally friendly transportation system that provides a high level of mobility and safety.

Imagine a city in which all vehicle movements (public and private) are scheduled and monitored in much the same way as the air traffic control system. Imagine a city in which you apply for access to (and use of) the series of roadways leading from your origin to your destination prior to your departure. While this concept is similar to that of the air traffic control system, in that your application permits pre-planning for the flow on each roadway, it differs in the sense that it does not assign the motorist a specific slot in the traffic stream. Entry and exit to traffic flows, as well as driving speeds on each roadway, would be determined by each driver. Transit trips would be prescheduled in much the same manner, with the traveler identifying the transit vehicles to be used, at which time the cost of the trip would be provided and the traveler's account would be debited.

Travelers would be billed while en route for access to the transportation system depending on the mode, time of day, and existing levels of demand. Since trips are prescheduled, transit vehicle arrivals and departures would be adjusted based on demand, traffic signal timing would have been calculated in advance, and travelers will be guaranteed access to the desired roadways and/or transit facilities. Each time a trip is made, the schedule, including mass transit arrival and departure times and costs, is displayed and printed. Scheduling and payment of fees (including parking and loading docks) is required of all vehicles including trucks, cars, and mass transit vehicles. Using a variable pricing structure determined dynamically, both time-of-day and mode choice will be influenced. Software applications would be used that *learn* the elasticity of demand under specific sets of conditions (weather, time-of-day, day-of-week, holidays, etc.) to ensure that pricing consistently produces the appropriate levels of demand for use of the transportation facilities. These applications would consider not only the capacity of the roadway infrastructure but also air quality. Thus on days where weather conditions result in a high likelihood of poor air quality, the pricing strategy would be adjusted for reduced travel demand using personal autos.

Payment for services would be highly automated, based on smartcards that can be used to purchase and schedule trips either through a personal computer or at kiosks located throughout the city. Smartcards are used for entry onto transit vehicles and inserted in a holster-type device (described below) in automobiles and trucks. The cards used in automobiles and trucks would be debited as roadside readers are passed. Charges would be adjusted based on a series of considerations programmed into the smartcard, such as income level, age, disabilities, and so on. In this way, the special needs of select groups can be accommodated.

Both commercial and private vehicles (including transit) would be equipped with a device that accepts smart cards that would be automatically debited for trips made within the urban area. The device will also incorporate a Global Positioning System (GPS) location capability and an emergency transmitter to be used for emergencies. Thus, with the exception of the smart card, the device will operate like many other onboard vehicle accessories such as the General Motors OnStar system, incorporating the capability for transmission of emergency information along with its location.

The system of the future incorporates radio transceivers at each intersection that monitor the locations and speeds of all vehicles using data transmitted from the onboard units. All vehicles using the transportation system would be required to contain the smart cards. This full market penetration, as well as its advanced reservation features, will guarantee effective adaptive signal control as well as immediate knowledge of any incidents or other disruptions to traffic flow. There is no need for the use of conventional vehicle detectors since the high level of market penetration of the onboard units will permit the data produced by these devices to be used for measuring vehicle flow rates as well as speeds and travel times.

A number of other surveillance technologies will be employed in addition to the use of onboard equipment. These include extensive closed circuit television (CCTV) coverage of both the roadway and pedestrian levels of activity. CCTV coverage will be used for both security and incident monitoring purposes. Air quality monitors, weather stations, and pavement sensors would be installed throughout the region for the previously mentioned purpose of adjusting traffic demand and flow through the use of adaptive pricing strategies, as well as for input to the adaptive traffic signal control system.

The technology and pricing strategies described here are similar to the VMT pricing scheme described in Chapter 5, in a negative way. The difference between these strategies and the VMT pricing strategy is that there are many other benefits to the motorist in terms of improved travel times and uncongested roadways. The approach described here also eliminates the need for special equipment at gas stations or other locations installed for billing purposes.

This vision isn't as crazy as it sounds, since the ingredients of the system either exist or are under development. For example, onboard electronics capable of measuring vehicle speed and location already exist. All that is missing is the will to use them. Smart cards and other similar devices that charge a fee based on the use of facilities are already in operation. A research project funded by the U.S. Department of Transportation, initially known as vehicle infrastructure integration (VII) and subsequently renamed and modified as IntelliDrive, contains many of the features that have been described. More about this later.

The Twenty-First-Century Highway

As any meteorologist can tell you, predicting the future can be a risky business . . . and the more distant the prediction, the greater the risk. The preceding two examples have minimized this risk in that they are developed around existing technologies. Even without the emergence of new currently unknown capabilities, it is possible to create a twenty-first-century highway system. All that is needed is the will to do it. The ingredients needed to move from today's system to the system of the future are discussed in the remaining chapters.

Futurists might wonder about the absence of the Automated Highway System (AHS) from these descriptions. In case you are not already familiar with the AHS, it is one in which the car (or truck) drives itself. There are many potential benefits to be realized from such a system, including greatly increased safety, higher potential speeds, and greater roadway capacity. The increased capacity is achieved by permitting vehicles to follow each other much more closely than is possible with human drivers since the faster reaction time of an automated system as well as improved knowledge of downstream conditions greatly reduces the possibility of rear end collisions.

But there are many technical challenges associated with a fully automated system. While in theory such a system produces tremendous benefits, it does so only when all of the vehicles in the traffic stream are working perfectly. Perfectly includes the absence of mechanical, electrical, and software failures. Anyone who owns a personal computer is familiar with the occasional situation in which the computer freezes and has to be rebooted. Imagine traveling at eighty miles per hour when the software in your car freezes and has to be rebooted. Not a comfortable situation.

So at the risk of appearing too conservative, AHS has been eliminated as a near-term possibility for the twenty-first-century highway system. My forecast is that it will make its appearance during the latter half of the century.

CHAPTER 9

Developing the Workforce

None of us is as smart as all of us.
—Ken Blanchard[71]

~~~~~~~~~~~~~~~~~~~~~~~~~~~~~~~~~

IT DOES NO GOOD TO WHINE ABOUT THE CURRENT state of affairs without offering some practical solutions to the problem. After forty years in the business and much contemplation on this subject, it appears that these solutions require a three-pronged attack. The ingredients of this attack discussed in these concluding chapters are within our grasp. All that is required is the will to move forward. The three prongs include:

1. Workforce development: Solutions cannot be implemented without the presence of an educated and committed cadre of individuals capable of moving the process forward. Workforce development is the subject of this chapter.
2. Organization: As used here, organization obviously includes the public transportation agencies themselves but also the political processes that control the manner in which the highway system is funded and managed. Should these organizations be replaced, reorganized, or reenergized?
3. Technology: The tools exist for an aggressive proactive approach to transportation management and operations. As discussed in the near-term vision of the preceding chapter, the private sector (including the automobile industry) is already implementing many of these changes.

It's time for the public sector to catch up. However, they cannot catch up without the workforce, organization, and will to support their efforts.

What is Workforce Development?

Several years ago during an informal discussion at a meeting of the AASHTO subcommittee on systems operation and management (SSOM), the participants pointed out that efforts to increase the emphasis on M&O were doomed to failure until adequately trained professional staff was available. Those participating in the discussion included high-ranking state transportation officials, including one secretary of transportation, all of whom indicated that they were trying to move away from the construction mentality but were hamstrung by the absence of personnel with the needed credentials. The Operations Academy was an outgrowth of that discussion.

The Operations Academy is sponsored by the University of Maryland. It is intended to provide an M&O orientation to senior level transportation and law enforcement professionals employed by state and local agencies.[72] Through a two week, total immersion program, the academy provides training to individuals throughout the United States on the subject of highway transportation management and operations. One or two sessions are scheduled annually for an average class size of twenty-five individuals. To date, nearly two hundred individuals have attended the academy, and demand continues to increase. The academy provides some education on the technical aspects of M&O but highlights management issues such as performance measurement, customer service, planning, and change management. Attendees visit traffic management centers and network with each other to discuss promising M&O activities of their own agencies. If the degree to which networking continues following the conclusion of the session is any indicator, the academy has proved to be a rewarding experience for all attendees. Thus, during the past six years, the academy has produced more than two hundred devotees to the field of M&O—individuals committed to improving the utilization of today's highway system and presumably anxious to make the transition from the highway system of the twentieth century to that of the twenty-first century.

If we are to overcome the inertia of the past as described by the preceding chapters, it is essential to replicate and expand the activities of the Operations Academy many times. It is necessary to develop a cadre of individuals holding senior positions within transportation agencies who *get it*. It is also necessary to develop academic programs at the university level so that appropriately trained individuals can be fed into the system on a continuing basis. The challenge is to both entice talented individuals into the field of transportation M&O and to identify the needed knowledge, skills, and abilities (KSAs) required to accomplish this goal.

Attracting the Workforce

It makes no sense to invest in the development of an M&O workforce if no one shows up to the party. Thus, the first step in workforce development is the attraction of large numbers of talented individuals to the field of transportation M&O.

Civil engineering is generally considered to be the profession from which M&O personnel are drawn. The educational programs of many universities throughout the United States include courses related to M&O, including subjects such as traffic flow theory and traffic control technology. Yet according to Wikipedia, "Civil engineering is a professional engineering discipline that deals with the design, construction, and maintenance of the physical and naturally built environment, including works such as bridges, roads, canals, dams, and buildings."[73] Note that there is no mention of activities associated with the effective utilization of these same physical works (M&O). As a result, it should not be surprising that few students considering an engineering career give serious consideration to M&O. Why would they? Even if transportation management and operations was a well-known and respected profession, conventional wisdom has it that this type of career is not very exciting when compared with the thrill of association with a major civil works project such as the design and construction of a major bridge or dam.

But the conventional wisdom is wrong. M&O can be a fascinating career if sold properly to the correct audience. Several years ago, I was discussing my profession with a neighbor whose husband was a high-ranking civilian official within the Department of Defense who managed a program nearly equal to the budget of a state DOT. Her reaction to the description of my work was "I wish my husband was involved in such fascinating work. You really make a difference in people's everyday lives. I can understand what you do but only have a vague notion of my husband's work."

And if that isn't enough, consider the range of disciplines and skills required to support an M&O activity, which include both technical and non-technical subjects. The list of required skills is impressive. The needed skills span a variety of engineering (civil, traffic, electrical, and mechanical), mathematics (operations research and statistics at least), computer science (software development, database management, computer engineering), geography, political science, human factors, project management, public policy, and business-related disciplines. Thus, the problem of increasing the size of the M&O workforce is a mixed blessing since on the one hand it includes a fascinating range of disciplines, but at the same time it complicates the workforce training process. Many consider this to be an attractive feature of the field since one never runs out of new things in which to participate.

Recognizing the breadth of the M&O field, I suggested that the University of Maryland should broaden its transportation engineering program to include additional IT-related subjects as it currently existed within the Civil Engineering (CE) Department. To my surprise, the reaction was one of concern that if CE students were to become too conversant with computer-related subjects, they would migrate out of the CE department into computer science. Rather than recognizing the potential of attracting computer science majors to transportation engineering, the inferiority complex of the CE faculty caused them to conclude that they should cloister their students to avoid losing them to another field. The CE profession needs to *get over* this concern.

Attracting a workforce should build on these more *sexy* aspects of the field. It should emphasize the variety of subjects involved and the opportunities to make a difference. Efforts should be made to attract students from the many associated specialties to the M&O field. Programs in which university faculty visit local high schools to attract upper classmen to their programs should also emphasize these points. At the present time, these programs tend to be narrow: CE faculty visit high schools to speak about CE, electrical engineering faculty tend to speak only about electrical engineering subjects, and so on. There are no programs in which multi-disciplinary careers such as transportation M&O are described, just as there are very few programs within the university system that accommodate the requirements of the profession. As a result, it is not surprising to hear the lament that occurred at the SSOM meeting, that there is no workforce to lead the M&O charge.

With the maturation of the M&O field, it is necessary to give serious consideration to workforce development, since the absence of adequate personnel will stifle its continued expansion. It is also necessary to recognize the parameters of the field in terms of its affiliated specialties as well as the types of education and training required. Perhaps most important, it is time to begin thinking creatively about techniques that might be used to attract additional professionals to consider a career in M&O. In short, it is time to stop whining about the shortage and begin to proactively correct the situation through a publicity campaign aimed at graduating high school seniors and undergraduate college students.

Integrating the M&O Workforce into the Existing System

After a cadre of M&O employees has been attracted to the transportation profession, additional problems emerge in the form of incompatibilities between the traditional transportation agency employee and the new breed of M&O employees. (No one said this would be easy.) The characteristics of these new employees are at odds with those of the traditional public sector workforce that is typically very stable with employees who remain with the agency for long time periods. Public sector employees tend to be conservative and are generally reluctant to take risks. On the other hand, employees in the field of electrical engineering and computer science tend to exhibit the following:

- Low level of employer loyalty: Because of the relative high demand for these specialties, along with the escalating technologies with which they are involved, they tend to have a high turnover rate and low employer loyalty. The average duration of employment within these fields is approximately two years. This is far less than the twenty- to thirty-year careers typical of public sector employees.
- Rate of technology advancement: High tech fields are changing rapidly. Electrical and computer science employees value opportunities for training and participation in relevant technical societies in order to keep up with these advances. If they feel that their current job is causing them to lag technically, they will relocate. The disconnect between technological advances in these professions as opposed to those in the traditional highway technologies was highlighted to me when the Transportation Research Board (TRB) contracted with Farradyne Systems (the company of my employment during the 1980s and 1990s) for a synthesis report on the use of telecommunications by transportation agencies. The telecommunications industry had advanced so much during the six-month TRB report review and publication cycle that major sections of the report had to be rewritten prior to its publication. Yet in the past, the six-month TRB cycle had been adequate for the more traditional transportation community.
- Salary: High technology jobs typically command extraordinarily high salaries that are rarely compatible with the public agency salary structure. This misalignment

of salaries among various technical specialties was particularly troublesome during the 1990s when the salaries of high tech employees were increasing at a rate of 10 percent to 15 percent per year while civil engineering salaries were increasing at a rate of 3 percent to 5 percent. During this same period, electrical engineers and computer programmers were commanding annual starting salaries of $60,000 to $80,000 while civil engineering salaries were $10,000 to $20,000 lower. Both public and private organizations employing high tech specialties experienced the predictable problems associated with inconsistent salary policies (jealousy, criticism, low morale, high turnover rates, etc.).

There is a feeling within the transportation profession that the technical issues are less difficult than the institutional problems associated with a given project or program. In spite of this recognized relationship, leaders of the M&O specialty fail to address the fundamental need for associated non-technical skills. A representative list of useful skills includes public policy, contracting, advertising, and human relations. Consider the following:

- Public policy becomes critical in an environment with shrinking revenue and increased costs combined with the need for alternatives to the fuel tax. How does M&O compete in this environment?
- Traditional use of the low-bid contracting procedure is inappropriate for high-tech projects. It is also inappropriate for selection of outsourcing contractors. An understanding of contracting alternatives and constraints is essential.
- Advertising and human relations have always been important and poorly addressed by the transportation community that relies on its technical specialists to sell its programs. Increased emphasis on public outreach to elected officials and the general public is more important in the M&O discipline where the absence of impressive physical structures and ribbon-cutting ceremonies requires effective outreach to sell its programs.

An example of the need for integrating these skills is the growing emphasis on performance measurement. Technical skills are needed for the collection and analysis of performance data. Management skills are required to facilitate public-private partnerships (P3s) related to the acquisition of performance-related data. At the same time, public policy and business skills are required to identify the needed measures and the most effective manner for their presentation to lay people, including the traveling public and elected officials. The absence of any of these skills will handicap the program.

Thus, a broad-based skilled workforce is essential to an effective M&O program. The absence of critical elements of the program can cripple its effectiveness. Public agencies seeking to expand their M&O program must identify the needed technical and non-technical skills, develop position descriptions for these skills, and develop a time-phased workforce development/ recruitment program to fill the necessary positions. It would be a mistake to let an M&O program evolve without an accompanying workforce development plan.

Finding the Workforce

Assuming that the budget exists to develop or expand an M&O workforce, where are the employees to be found? There are four obvious sources: new graduates (university, junior college, etc), retraining of existing employees, attracting employees from other organizations, or outsourcing (in the case of public agencies). Numerous factors influence the source of workforce employees, the most obvious being availability and budget constraints. The differences between these sources of employees in terms of prior experience, immediacy of need, and degree of mentoring required before they become effective are substantial. These decisions cannot be made until a workforce development plan has been prepared. Some important considerations include:

- New graduates: As noted in the following section, it is very difficult to recruit individuals from both the technical and non-technical specialties to the M&O

profession, which must compete with many other opportunities within and outside of transportation M&O. Extreme cases include the programmer with the job opportunity at GOOGLE or the talented advertising specialist with a job opportunity at Proctor and Gamble. It would be a rare situation if a transportation agency successfully competed with these types of opportunities. When competing with more glamorous industries, public agencies may need to abandon internal staff development and rely on consulting support. Even within the transportation profession, local agencies often find it difficult to compete with private sector salaries when attempting to attract new graduates.

- Retraining: Retraining may be a desirable option for those organizations faced with the option of potential layoffs in shrinking disciplines. Moving employees from an area with decreasing workforce requirements into an expanding area may be in the best interest of both the employee and the organization. For example, as construction budgets shrink, the need for skills associated with new roadways (design, construction management, environmental impact, etc.) decreases. However, effective cross training requires a genuine commitment and interest on the part of those being cross-trained, which may be difficult to achieve.

- Hiring: Attracting experienced employees from other organizations (agencies or the private sector) requires that the hiring organization offer a position that is more attractive than the existing position of the individual being courted. This includes salary, benefits, job security, opportunities for advancement, or most important— rewarding work assignments. With the exception of job security and benefits, these attractions may be difficult for a public agency to offer. For this reason, it is important that the workforce development plan include career track information to provide those with an appetite for advancement, the assurance that *there will be some place to go* if they were to join the organization.

- Outsourcing: Outsourcing is being increasingly used as an alternative to staff workforce development. However, it is important to recognize that the use of outsourcing does not relieve the agency of the need for an M&O workforce since it is important that the agency's needs be represented to the outsourced activity. In fact, increased use of outsourcing leads to a transition in the skills required by the agency. Instead of doing the work themselves, agency employees must now be familiar with competitive bidding processes, contracting, and overseeing the work of the contractor.

It is likely that the development and/or expansion of an M&O workforce will rely on all of these sources since the required skills are not universally available for all specialties from all sources.

Training the Workforce

The preparation of a workforce development plan is essential since each of the alternatives described here requires that differing actions be taken. The plan should identify employee(s) needed, including their knowledge and skills; the source(s) of new employees; both the source and type of training required; if outsourcing is used—the names of candidate firms that can provide the needed services, budget, and schedule. Many of these alternative sources of personnel take time to evolve. Thus, the workforce development plan is not a one-shot activity. It is an ongoing program that, in some cases, takes years before it bears results.

It is not uncommon for an organization to focus on the *ideal* employee as one who has five to ten years of experience with the specialty of the position it is trying to fill. Some organizations have spent five or more years trying to find that ideal employee. If they had invested the same time and effort on internal staff development, they would already have a workforce of *ideal* employees. Thus, a workforce development program should be accompanied by a training curriculum that permits the conversion of existing employees into the ideal employees that are needed. This suggestion is based on the premise that organizations will be able to establish training budgets and abandon the common practice of eliminating those budgets as soon as funding shortages occur. In other words, training budgets should not be considered a discretionary expense that can be used for a variety of optional purposes but rather an essential component of an agency's workforce development program. Training is the key to attracting new hires, as well as retraining of existing employees in this fast-moving field.

A number of sources exist for M&O training, including: the Operations Academy (www.operationsacademy.org), the Consortium for ITS Training and Education (www.citeconsortium. org), and traditional university programs. These various programs offer a bewildering array of training courses, college programs, and training styles (classroom versus online) that meet the needs of the variety of employment specialties associated with the M&O field. The recently completed National Cooperative Highway Research Program (NCHRP) project 20-77 cataloged all of the courses and programs available as of 2009 in the form of a database that permits the user to identify specific programs or to develop tailored training programs associated with specific specialties and positions. The NCHRP database includes all of the sources listed above. The database, which is accessible at www.catt.umd.edu/documents/NCHRPTraining-Framework.pdf permits the user to select the subject of interest and identifies all of the relevant training material.

It must be emphasized that today's employees consider training in a rapidly evolving field to be an essential employment benefit. It is less expensive to provide this benefit than to recruit new staff members. As a result, serious consideration must be given to the integration of an effective training program into the workforce development program.

Where Do the Universities Fit In?

The development of a trained workforce that is hired for entry-level positions at the bottom of the professional employment ladder is the domain of the universities. Unfortunately, there are many impediments to the development of a management and operations curriculum within the U.S. university system, not the least of which is the fact that the economy has forced many universities to reduce the number of degrees that they are offering, rather than expand. In addition, the expansion of a curriculum is a painful process that requires approvals up to the very top of the university management. It must be accompanied by justification of the need for the curriculum as well as evidence that the demand exists for this type of education. This is truly a daunting process that has stymied many other fields outside the transportation community.

A more desirable alternative would be to encourage universities to initiate a certificate program. The program offered by Princeton University is a representative example.[74] According to the Princeton website:

> Certificates of proficiency enable students to supplement their work in their departmental concentrations with focused study in another, often interdisciplinary, field. Certificate programs are similar in many ways to the minors offered at other universities.

A program of this nature is ideally suited to the needs of the M&O field in that it permits students specializing in transportation systems to address their interests in other subjects associated with management and operations. For example, students specializing in traffic engineering might choose political science or computer science as their interdisciplinary fields. At many universities, certificate programs are more readily developed since they are based on existing courses and only require the approval of the deans of the participating schools. These types of programs are also very popular with companies and government agencies seeking ongoing educational opportunities for their employees.

The steps to be taken toward the development of a robust national certificate program might include:

1. Definition of the range of ingredients that might be included in a certificate program. This might include

a model program that can be followed by universities interested in offering M&O Certificates.

2. Identification and nurturing of a group of universities related to the development of M&O certificate programs
3. Proactive encouragement of perspective undergraduates and working professionals to enroll in these programs
4. Working with both public and private sector organizations to convince them of the value of employing individuals with the appropriate certificates

These four steps are easily written but difficult to accomplish. It would be important for an organization such as the USDOT, through its various programs that provide financial support to universities, to pursue an aggressive workforce development program.

Some Final Thoughts about Workforce Development

The creation or expansion of an M&O workforce is not a trivial undertaking. Unlike the good old days when highway agencies and design companies were the only game in town, today's high tech employees have a smorgasbord of attractive alternatives to the traffic field. The odds of attracting and hiring qualified individuals must be improved. This cannot be done passively. It requires: (1) a marketing program in which junior college and college undergraduates are persuaded that M&O can be an attractive and rewarding career, (2) a workforce development plan that ensures that the necessary ingredients for attracting and retaining qualified employees is in place, and (3) an aggressive plan for the implementation of certificate programs at various universities throughout the United States. These plans must emphasize training opportunities, availability of career paths and ways in which salaries for M&O employees can be made compatible with those of other fields.

M&O is a relatively new and important facet of the highway transportation field. Its success can only be ensured with the availability of a qualified and inspired workforce.

CHAPTER 10

Technology—A Key to the Twenty-First Century

The wireless music box has no imaginable
commercial value. Who would pay for a
message sent to nobody in particular?
— David Sarnoff's Associates[75]

~~~~~~

What is the twenty-first-century highway? Two pictures of the future have been painted in attempt to define what it might be: The first was a near-term future that featured the dissemination of greatly enhanced information to the traveling public, and aggressive M&O performed by public agencies. The second, longer-term vision featured a highly managed highway system in which slots were reserved for travelers prior to their departure. Predicting the future is always a risky business because so many variables are involved. As a result, neither of these futures might be quite right, although the near-term forecast is undoubtedly close. But the common denominator of these two visions is the ubiquitous availability of information technology to facilitate their implementation. There is little doubt that when it arrives the backbone of the twenty-first-century highway system will be a powerful combination of data communications and information dissemination to travelers prior to their departure, while en route, and after reaching their destination. To use twenty-first-century terminology, the question is: what are the M&O apps that will emerge to take advantage of all this technology?

Programs That Began with Promise

During the 1990s, many ITS champions felt that the impacts of its widespread implementation would be equivalent to that of a second U.S. interstate system. In other words, these ITS champions viewed it as the path to the twenty-first-century highway system. Unfortunately, the technology was cautiously adopted on an as-needed basis, and the dream never materialized. It also failed to materialize because of the emphasis on technology (ITS) as opposed to its application (M&O).

The Automated Highway System Program

The AHS program was established in 1992 in an effort to *realize the dream*. The objective of this program was to enable vehicle operation without requiring human intervention. In other words, it embodied the creation of a highway with driverless vehicles, fulfilling the *Popular Science* magazine prophesies of the 1950s. AHS was an effort to leapfrog the gradual introduction of ITS technology by providing significant improvements in roadway safety and capacity. While it is easy to understand the concept of driverless cars, its implementation is much more difficult. The technology developed by this program had to operate reliably within the many different types of roadway and environmental conditions encountered by the typical automobile, it had to be a robust system that could accommodate potential failures of other vehicles within the system, and it required a level of software reliability that has not been achieved to this day.

While these problems may have been solvable, it was estimated that at least fifteen years would be required to complete the research and development needed to meet the challenges of AHS. As a result, the program was eventually cancelled by the USDOT in 1998 due to funding pressures and a feeling that the development of near-term safety systems should be given a higher priority. Undoubtedly, the inherent impatience of the political process that prefers near-term successes that can be integrated into congressional reelection campaigns also played a role in this decision.

Vehicle Infrastructure Integration

Research programs conducted both in parallel with the AHS and subsequent to its untimely conclusion offered alternative approaches to the use of technology to advance safety. In 2003, these programs coalesced into a major initiative then known as the Vehicle Infrastructure Integration (VII) program. VII took advantage of the extensive instrumentation installed in the modern automobile to measure speed, roadway and weather conditions, vehicle location, and direction. It was thought that the cumulative information received from the overall traffic stream could be an invaluable asset for both safety and traffic management applications. Twenty-first-century vehicles are very smart. They obviously know how fast they're going (the speedometer), they know where they are (GPS based navigation systems), they know if it is light or dark (automatic headlight activation), they know the temperature, they know whether the pavement is slippery (automatic braking systems or ABS), they know whether it is raining (windshield wipers), they know whether there are potholes to be repaired (suspension system), and so on. Some vehicles even know how close they are to the car in front of them or to a roadway obstruction. They also know if you are having difficulty staying in your lane and whether your air bag deployed. They might also know whether or not you are looking for parking or planning to eat at a nearby Chinese restaurant. And of course many vehicles are equipped with the ability to automatically pay tolls, a feature that could readily be expanded to include payment for parking, gasoline, and other travel services.

If even a small percentage of the total vehicles on a given road were equipped to send all their knowledge to a central site, imagine what might be accomplished. Authorities could immediately sense that an airbag had deployed and dispatch emergency assistance.[76] System operators could assess the speeds of vehicles on various routes and provide alternate routing information to motorists. The impending arrival of a platoon of vehicles at a downstream intersection could be used to automatically adjust the traffic signal timing so that the signal would turn green as the platoon arrived. The presence of potholes would automatically be detected so that they could be rapidly patched before causing an accident or damaging vehicles. Highly accurate maps of roadways could be developed, improving the quality of navigation systems and permitting the development of reliable lane departure warning systems that alert the driver when he is wandering out of his lane. Maintenance personnel could automatically be alerted to the presence of ice so that sand and salt trucks can be dispatched. More important, other drivers could be warned of the hazardous conditions as they approach the slippery pavement. The list is only limited by the imagination in the same way that the apps developed for various handheld devices such as the iPod and Android are proliferating.

Perhaps more significant is the fact that these same systems could significantly reduce crashes at intersections and other hazardous locations. Knowing the positions and speeds of vehicles approaching an intersection, it is possible to predict the possibility of an intersection collision and command one or both of the vehicles to take evasive action. For example, in the city of Albuquerque, New Mexico alone, there are nearly 5,000 intersection crashes per year (for an average of nearly fourteen crashes per day). A reduction in the number of intersection crashes, by itself, could justify the entire cost of a program that takes advantage of the intelligence of the twenty-first-century vehicles.

The VII program was created within the USDOT with the objective of integrating these capabilities. The unstated objective of this program was the use of IT technology to create the new electronic interstate. The benefits of the program in terms of improved safety and mobility for the traveling public were obvious: improved safety through the reduction of intersection collisions and more rapid response to crashes and significantly enhanced mobility due to improved signal timing, ramp metering, and diversion under conditions that require the knowledge of traffic demand on all roadways.

The USDOT recognized that the implementation of such an ambitious program required the participation and collaboration of many sectors of the transportation community, including the public sector departments of transportation and local departments of public works, the private sector automobile manufacturers and consultants, and various equipment manufacturers. All participants agreed that this was a significant groundbreaking program. After many years of development, definition of the VII program should have been an easy task. Unfortunately, due to the number and variety of participants, there was little consensus on many aspects of the system, particularly the business model by which it would be constructed and operated. Participants providing planning and guidance for VII included various segments of the USDOT (Joint Program Office, highway operations, safety, transit, and motor carriers), state governments, the automobile industry, aftermarket equipment manufacturers, communications providers, navigation and traffic information providers, and many others. Considering the number and diversity of interested parties, it should not be surprising that consensus was difficult to achieve. After much debate, general agreement was reached that in addition to the emphasis on safety and mobility, the system should support electronic payment applications (tolls, parking, etc.), commercial in-vehicle services (restaurant reservations, fast food orders, in-vehicle banking, etc.), and support various automobile industry requirements such as remote diagnostics of vehicle operation.

These objectives were ultimately translated into the system architecture shown in Figure 6 that featured two-way communications between the vehicle and a roadside unit using a protocol known as dedicated short range communication (DSRC). The roadside units (RSUs) receive data from the vehicles that is then communicated through routers (not shown in the diagram). The routers then direct the appropriate vehicle data to large databases with temporary storage that is used by a variety of applications. Not shown in the diagram is the vehicle-to-vehicle communications required for multiple vehicle crash avoidance such as right angle accidents at intersections involving two vehicles. In other words, the VII architecture relied on the installation of roadside units (RSUs) at frequent intervals along freeways and at all major signalized intersections to extract the needed data from the onboard units (OBUs) installed in the passing vehicles.

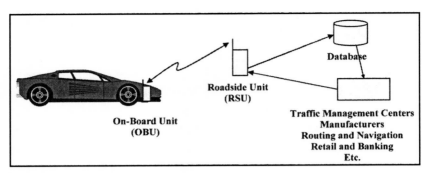

FIGURE 6   VII Architecture

Imagine the safety improvements possible if either the driver or the vehicle knew that there was the chance of an imminent crash due to the presence of other vehicles or that vehicle speed was too high for slippery pavement or sharp curves, or that the driver was deviating from the travel lane due to inattention or impairment. The promise of VII is a significant reduction in the six million crashes occurring in the United States each year at a direct economic cost of more than $230 billion (in 2000 dollars).[77] The VII program was intended to reduce vehicle crashes by 90 percent by 2030.[78] If this goal had been met, the economic savings of reduced crashes would have more than offset the estimated $6 billion cost of the system. Unfortunately, similar goals were never established for the mobility and commercial benefits of the system.

In spite of its potential benefits, things did not go well with the VII program for a variety of significant reasons, not least of which is the impatience of the federal bureaucracy with long-term research. Programs lasting more than four or five years have a difficult time obtaining continuing funding unless they produce significant results. The need to obtain the consensus of the multi-faceted working group before moving forward was also a problem. It is difficult to move forward with an imaginative system design when the leadership is hampered by conflicting motivations found in a group of this nature.

Perhaps the most significant reason for the program's lack of success was its design. The architecture described here could not be developed incrementally. The system required the nationwide installation of RSUs in order for the auto manufacturers to justify their investment in the in-vehicle OBUs. Since automobiles are driven throughout the country, it would not be sufficient to install in-vehicle OBUs that would only work in the New England states, for example. The estimated cost of this nationwide network of unproven features was approximately $6 billion, a difficult funding hurdle in an uncertain economy at a time when the overall highway system was already experiencing significant financial shortages.

You might ask why an architecture requiring national installation of roadside units was selected. For example, why couldn't satellite communication or some other form of wireless communication be used that relied on existing communications networks? This architecture was dictated by the inclusion of safety features intended to prevent multi-vehicle intersection collisions. These types of features require that communications between two vehicles approaching an intersection be established within a few hundredths of a second (a characteristic known as latency), a requirement that exceeded the capabilities of any existing commercial service. Thus a single feature (albeit an important one) drove the entire architecture for the program, an architecture that may have led to its demise.

VII was ultimately reconstituted into a new program known as IntelliDrive that was renamed again, as the Connected Vehicle Research program. IntelliDrive is not discussed here since it is little more than a collection of projects involving standards, relatively narrow safety research, and training, operating under a common name. It does not offer the same potential of revolutionizing the twentieth-century highway system.

The Common Denominator

The demise of AHS and the reconstitution of VII raise the obvious question: is the federal government capable of leading the modernization of the U.S. highway system? The lack of success of these two programs, as well as several others not described here, suggests that there are fundamental obstacles associated with a federally led program that are difficult if not impossible to overcome.

First is the absence of agility. Structurally, it is impossible for the federal government to act quickly and change direction as dictated by unanticipated obstacles and/or the appearance of new technologies. Federal programs require the approval of senior managers and in some cases elected officials. Once such approval is obtained, it is difficult to make changes in program direction without undergoing the unpleasant (for a bureaucrat) process of reeducation and rejustification. To make matters worse, national highway programs require the concurrence of the fifty state DOTs, since after all, they are the owners of the highway system. If the program affects the automobile industry, further concurrence and collaboration is required from the major manufacturers, as well as their after-market suppliers. If the program affects local roadways, concurrence is also required from cities and counties. The chance of receiving the acceptance for any program by a majority of these participants, each of which having their own agenda, is remote at best. Nothing could be more applicable than the saying that a camel is a horse designed by a committee. If the current processes were to be followed, the required levels of concurrence and collaboration would undoubtedly lead to a twenty-first-century highway system that looks like a camel.

The second obstacle is the public sector's penchant for control. Federal employees within agencies such as the FHWA within USDOT correctly feel that they are the guardians of the tax dollars being spent on programs within their purview. As a result, they manage major programs such as VII with a heavy hand. The shaping process includes control over the architecture, data standards, data utilization, contractor selection, and so on. They ensure that minority businesses receive a fair share of the work, that all procurements are competitive, and that all investments are successful. While this is a logical extension of public sector responsibilities, it prevents innovation and eliminates the agility required by a high tech development. It is impossible for a public agency to manage the evolutionary development of new capabilities involving dozens of competing firms offering dazzling new technologies. Could you imagine the federal government managing the competing development of the cellular telephone system and its associated devices such as the iPhone and Android?

But there are successful alternatives . . .

A Success Story

Effective M&O cannot be performed without knowledge of the traffic that is being managed. To manage traffic without adequate information is analogous to installing a home heating system without a thermostat. The operation of the furnace would be completely independent of the temperature of the house but would rely on manual intervention based on personal impressions of hot or cold. Yet until recently, the operators of our twentieth-century highway system attempted to manage traffic flow without any up-to-date knowledge of traffic conditions. They based their decisions on cell phone calls from motorists, occasional radio reports from field personnel, or information gleaned from scattered television cameras. In short, they managed the system based on personal impressions. If all else failed, they based their decisions on historically collected data.

But this situation is changing. As a result of the availability of new technology and new business models, M&O appears to be on the threshold of a traffic monitoring revolution. The possibility of pervasive traffic monitoring offers the opportunity for the dissemination of reliable traveler information and effective traffic management, truly a paradigm shift in our current processes and a first step toward the twenty-first-century highway system, a step that appears to be led by developments in the private sector, in which the public sector only plays a supporting role.

Both new and existing companies have long recognized the increasing demand for travel time information. At least in part, this demand has been stimulated by the popularity of the navigation devices offered both as original equipment and aftermarket devices. The ubiquitous availability of travel time information from navigation devices improves the utility (and presumably the sales) of these units, which can now provide routes to the user that take current travel times into account. It goes without saying that the nationwide collection of real-time travel time data is an expensive undertaking. It was not until the advent of inexpensive navigation devices of the type offered by Garmin, Magellan, TomTom, and location-equipped cell phones that the market has grown to a size adequate to support this investment. The market has become even more attractive with the development of routing apps that also offer routing information based on real-time traffic information. The revenue produced by this market is far in excess of $100 million per year.

As a result, a growing list of companies with names such as Airsage, Calmar, INRIX, Speedinfo, and Traffic.com are offering travel time information in electronic formats for use in navigation devices and at the same time to public agencies and the media for their own traveler information and traffic management applications.

One particularly interesting technology is that of INRIX, Inc. that tracks the location of vehicles in GPS-equipped fleets, as well as the positions of vehicles with navigation devices whose users have agreed to have their location sampled on a periodic basis. INRIX translates this location data into speeds and travel times for the routes that the tracked vehicles are using. The data is also offered to the public sector transportation agencies at a cost of approximately $750 per mile per year, a cost that is less than these agencies would spend to collect the same information using their own dedicated equipment.

Other technologies in addition to INRIX's GPS-based information are in use. One is based on the installation of various types of speed detectors at periodic locations along the roadside. Cell phone geolocation that tracks the locations of cell phone users at periodic intervals in order to determine the speed of their vehicles is another technology that has been employed for the derivation of travel time and speeds. This rich mix of technologies and the growing list of entrepreneurial companies are having a significant impact on the public sector transportation community. In essence, this community is beginning to recognize the value of purchasing services from the private sector instead of trying to do it all themselves.

Transportation agencies have long recognized the potential of high-quality traffic flow data but have resisted the installation of conventional vehicle detectors due to their cost. With reduced cost and increased demand for travel information, a number of statewide and regional monitoring projects have emerged—in most cases based on the acquisition of data from third-party providers. Because of the rate at which these projects are being initiated, it is not possible to provide a comprehensive list of the agencies pursuing this technology. However, even a partial list is impressive. In addition to the early adopters in Maryland, Virginia, Texas, and the New York metropolitan area, it includes states such as California, Georgia, Missouri, and Wisconsin. One of the most significant projects is being led by the I-95 Corridor Coalition, which recently executed a contract with INRIX Inc. for the acquisition of probe-based data along the I-95 corridor to acquire traffic flow data for six states including: New Jersey, Pennsylvania, Delaware, Maryland, Virginia, and North Carolina with other agencies. This contract was subsequently expanded by the Coalition to provide data along the I-95 Corridor for most of the states on the east coast.

The Moral of the Story

The significance of this success story is that a major step has been made toward the evolution of the twenty-first-century highway system as a result of private sector initiatives. If additional successes are to occur, the public sector must foster an environment that encourages future developments of this nature.

Fostering Private Sector Participation

The first question to be answered is whether there are private sector opportunities within the transportation marketplace for which revenue sources exist that are equivalent to that of travel-time services business? In other words, are there technologies with adequate business potential to attract private industry investment in a way that will ensure the emergence of a twenty-first-century highway system? The answer to this question is not the sole domain of the author of this book but should be left to a nation of entrepreneurs eagerly searching for ways in which to apply their business and technical creativity.

In the absence of inputs from these hypothetical entrepreneurs, a few possibilities (some of which are radical in today's world) can be suggested:

1. Intersection ownership—in July 2001, State Farm Insurance, the nation's largest auto insurer, announced that it had identified the ten most dangerous U.S. intersections. This list was developed using the company's database of accident claims. State Farm offered municipalities in which these intersections were located grants of up to $120,000 for engineering studies and intersection upgrades. Presumably, State Farm initiated this program for two reasons. The good publicity associated with the funding of infrastructure improvements, and the possibility of reduced insurance claims resulting from safer intersections. Thus, in a small way, the private sector had assumed a role that should have been a public sector responsibility. As a small step toward the twenty-first-century highway system, why not hold an intersection auction for the insurance industry and other interested parties, in which successful bidders would assume ownerships of unsafe or highly congested intersections? The purchaser's reward would be posting the name of the intersection's owners in the same way in which the successful Adopt a Highway program provides organizations with the ability to advertise the fact that they are responsible for cleaning up a section of roadway. Giving credit to intersection owners would also ensure that owners would live up to their commitments to improved intersection operation.

2. Toll roads—the construction and operation of private toll roads has already been discussed. In high traffic areas, toll roads (including those that incorporate congestion pricing) generate adequate revenue to be self-supporting. As previously indicated, private toll roads represent a

return to the nineteenth-century concept, although this time, the roads would be constructed and operated to twenty-first-century standards.

3. In-vehicle signing—twenty-first-century vehicles are increasingly being equipped with sophisticated in-vehicle displays for navigation as well as interacting with other vehicle functions, to the point that within the next five years it would be unusual to purchase a new vehicle that did not include heating/cooling, radio, engine status, and navigation functions on a single integrated graphical display. Why not collocate radio transmitters with all highway signs? The radio transmitters would send the information (also contained on the sign) to passing vehicles for display on their integrated graphical displays. In the long term, when all vehicles are suitably equipped, this might lead to the complete replacement of existing highway signs with in-vehicle signing. In the short term, it would lead to improved readability by drivers of suitably equipped vehicles as well as the ability to transmit longer messages than those that can be effectively displayed on traditional signs. The private sector, including both auto manufacturers and after-market providers, might generate revenue from the provision of this capability that could be used in part for funding the installation of the needed collocated transmitters. As an alternative to the potentially distracting graphical displays, the sign messages could be provided to drivers in audio form.

4. Adaptive traffic signal control—one of the technologies in which the United States lags behind the rest of the world is that of adaptive signal control. This is a technology that replaces the old-fashioned time-clock operation currently in use with traffic signal timing that is automatically adjusted to be responsive to projected traffic demand. Why not offer ownership of the traffic signal system to the private sector along with incentive payments in which the private sector company is compensated for reductions in delays and improvements in travel time experienced by users of

the roadways on which the signals are installed. It must be emphasized that this is a tricky concept, in that the private sector must be required to guarantee high levels of reliability and must also be protected against lawsuits (some of which are frivolous) that occur at signalized intersections. It also requires a carefully crafted formula for measuring improvements; they may be difficult to achieve in locations experiencing increases in traffic demand.

And the list goes on. Opportunities are limited by the imagination, and not all ideas are equally practical.

Acquiring the New Technology

The preceding list was developed to demonstrate the range of possibilities that exist for private sector participation in the modernization of the twentieth-century highway system. The examples provided in this list demonstrate that the technology needed by the twenty-first-century highway system is not acquired through glacially moving government programs but rather by harnessing the creativity of American entrepreneurs. Moving to the twenty-first-century highway requires removal of potential obstacles and creation of incentives to encourage private sector participation.

In some cases, enabling legislation is needed to accomplish these goals. Legislation might be required to legalize the transfer of public facilities such as traffic signal systems and/or dangerous intersections to private sector ownership. Additional legislation might be required to permit the negotiation of incentive contracts in which companies are rewarded financially based on improvements that have been made to the quality of travel. In some states, it might also be necessary to introduce legislation to limit the liability of companies that have assumed direct responsibility for the operation of the system. However, these issues have been successfully addressed in the past (e.g., private ownership of toll roads), and can certainly be resolved in the future.

In the meantime, smaller initial steps can be taken through actions such as the use of design competitions that allow private sector firms to offer competing technologies and consideration of the outsourcing of various M&O functions to the private sector as discussed in the following chapter. The federal government can further encourage this process through the expansion and streamlining of existing programs that provide seed money for the development of promising technologies. There are similar programs currently in existence,[79] but they are limited and tend to carry an unpleasant bureaucratic burden.

In short, it is up to the public sector to proactively explore ways in which the development of new technology can be encouraged. At the same time, various approaches must be developed to accelerate the rate at which the new technology is incorporated into the highway system. Many success stories exist both within and without the highway industry, but it is essential that the exploration process include representatives of both the public and private sectors.

CHAPTER 11

Reorganizing the Dot—Revolution or Evolution

*Once an organization loses its spirit of
pioneering and rests on its early work, its
progress stops.*
— Thomas Watson, Sr.[80]

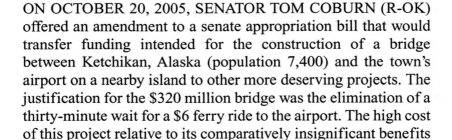

ON OCTOBER 20, 2005, SENATOR TOM COBURN (R-OK) offered an amendment to a senate appropriation bill that would transfer funding intended for the construction of a bridge between Ketchikan, Alaska (population 7,400) and the town's airport on a nearby island to other more deserving projects. The justification for the $320 million bridge was the elimination of a thirty-minute wait for a $6 ferry ride to the airport. The high cost of this project relative to its comparatively insignificant benefits led to its identification as a symbol of irresponsible pork barrel spending by members of congress. The bridge quickly became known derisively as the bridge to nowhere.

This story would be humorous if it were an isolated incident, but similar examples abound. Another pork barrel project of ridicule is I-99, the Bud Shuster Highway that runs through mountainous terrain from Bedford, Pennsylvania near the Pennsylvania turnpike to Bellefonte, Pennsylvania (north of State College, the home of Penn State University) for nearly eighty-six miles. It is difficult to determine the exact cost of this four-lane interstate since the roadway was constructed in many sections over a period of thirty years and involved very expensive environmental remediation to control runoff and potential groundwater contamination. But undoubtedly, the total cost of this interstate was many times the estimated cost of the bridge to nowhere. In essence, many hundreds of millions of dollars were spent to connect Bedford, a town with a population slightly in excess of 3,000, with the State College region whose population is approximately 136,000. The largest town served by I-99 is Scranton, Pennsylvania with its shrinking population of 72,000. Thus, an expensive four-lane interstate roadway was constructed through difficult mountainous terrain to serve a rural area of central Pennsylvania. It is undoubtedly not a coincidence that I-99 was named after Bud Shuster, a fourteen-term Pennsylvania congressman and undoubtedly contributed to his political success. A roadway serving a total population of approximately 200,000 individuals was constructed at a time when the United States was and still is struggling to provide adequate transportation for millions of people in the congested areas surrounding major metropolitan areas.

These examples could be repeated many times to describe annual pork barrel expenditures amounting to billions of dollars. It is clear that the time has come to disconnect the feeding tube known as the highway trust fund from the political interests of those who have been elected to serve the people. These examples have been offered at the beginning of a chapter discussing organizational alternatives to make the point that the best structural changes to the transportation system are those that reduce the impacts of political influence. This criterion is offered in recognition of the fact that political influence can never be completely removed from highway system planning process. Nor should it be removed. The political process ensures that the public's needs are satisfied and that compromises among those with competing viewpoints are satisfactorily reached.

Today's transportation system is beset by a host of problems in addition to political influence, including funding shortages, an upside down system of financing that rewards poor performance with increased money, inadequate attention to management and operations, absence of performance measurement, and failures to embrace new technology. The need for systemic changes is obvious. However, the nature of the changes is open to debate.

In the broadest sense, there are two alternative approaches to restructuring the transportation system, both of which include increased reliance on the private sector: (1) the revolutionary alternative in which existing agencies are eliminated and replaced by quasi-private sector franchises similar to that of a public utility, and (2) the evolutionary alternative in which existing agencies are restructured with a healthy dose of private sector outsourcing. There is a possible third alternative, not discussed here, that could be called the do-nothing alternative, the result of which is the continued operation of our inadequate twentieth-century highway system.

Much of the discussion in this and other chapters has compared public sector activities with those of the private sector. Don't be misled into thinking that the private sector is inherently smarter or more effective than the public sector. I am a believer in the saying that while the private sector is critical of the public sector, the first thing that a private sector company does when it gets big is to imitate the public sector. So the inefficiencies borne of bureaucracy and lower risk tolerance do not depend on whether an organization is public or private but rather its size. A book could be written on this subject alone. The emphasis on an increased role for the private sector as discussed here reflects its ability to reward private sector participants for good performance, to establish flexible staffing policies, minimize political pressures, and invest in performance measurement. As a result, there is much to recommend a significantly expanded role for the private sector in the management and operation of the twenty-first-century transportation system.

The Revolution—Agency Privatization

In February 2009, the Middle Atlantic states experienced a record snowstorm. When the storm ended, there was nearly four feet of snow on the ground in the Washington, DC area. Government agencies and utilities were swamped with clearing roads, restoring electrical power, and attending to the needs of the elderly and disabled. More than 100,000 homes were without power in the Maryland suburbs, and the Potomac Electric Power Company (PEPCO) struggled for more than a week to restore service to the region. The political establishment immediately leapt into action with a campaign of public humiliation, chastising PEPCO's management for the slow pace of power restoration. PEPCO's performance was compared with that of other utilities and was found wanting. In January 2010, the Maryland Public Service Commission requested authority to levy fines against PEPCO and other Maryland utilities if they fail to meet standards for reliability and customer service established by the commission.[81] The proposed requirements, which are contained in a notice of initiating rulemaking, are excerpted and summarized in Table 6 along with a parallel set of rules that could have been used by and for the transportation community.[82]

Category of Requirement	PSC Requirement	Hypothetical Transportation Requirement
Service Interruption Standards	For both normal and major events, restore service within 36 hrs. 90% of the time	For all types of incidents, open the roadway within 45 minutes 90% of the time
	For major events, restore service within 60 hrs. 90% of the time	For major incidents, open the roadway within two hours 90% of the time
		For major incidents involving natural events (snow, floods, etc.) open the roadway within three hours 90% of the time
	For normal conditions, restore service within 8 hrs. 90% of the time.	For other than major incidents, open the roadway within 20 minutes 90% of the time
Repairs	For both normal and major events, the repairs shall be performed within 240 minutes after notification 90% of the time.	For both normal and major roadway damages, repairs shall be completed and traffic restored within 240 minutes following notification 90% of the time.
Response to Customers	The average customer telephone call answer time shall be less than 90 seconds: or	Transportation agencies shall have a customer service hotline and shall answer in 90 seconds or less
	An electric utility shall have a telephone call response factor of 5% or less	Transportation agencies shall respond to at least 95% of call-in requests

TABLE 6   Comparison of PSC and Transportation Performance Criteria

The irony of the PEPCO criticism was that there was no similar discussion of the government's performance. How did snow plowing and incident response compare with that of other transportation agencies? How long did it take to restore the transportation system to full operation? Is it surprising that the subject was never discussed by the local politicians? You shouldn't be too surprised since the public transportation agencies do not measure their own performance, and even if they did, there are no standardized measures by which this performance can be compared with that of other agencies. The bottom line is that public officials do not want their own performance evaluated. They would prefer to criticize the performance of others. Restating this in a more positive way, perhaps the transportation system would best be managed by the private sector with governmental oversight (aka criticism) to ensure that adequate services are being delivered to the traveling public. If this were to occur, requirements such as those suggested by the third column of Table 6 might exist.

But the example of the snowstorm is an extreme one. Perhaps it would be instructive to examine the actions of the New York State Public Services Commission (PSC) in connection with regulation of their utilities. A recent news announcement indicated that the PSC tracked the performance of all of the state's utilities. It concluded that during 2009, service provided by the majority of utilities had met or exceeded performance standards for forty-eight of forty-nine measures. However, the performance of the New York State Electric and Gas Corporation failed to meet their performance targets, which resulted in an earnings reduction (fine) of $2.3 million.[83] The two most important of the forty-nine measures used by the PSC are the system average interruption frequency index (SAIFI) and the customer average interruption duration index (CAIDI). The SAIFI is the average number of times that a customer is interrupted during a year, while the CAIDI is the average duration time of an interruption for those customers that experienced an interruption.[84]

In the transportation world, this would be equivalent to determining how many motorists experienced delays due to an incident and the average duration of those delays. If New York were to provide a balanced program of service delivery, it would be reasonable to expect that the level of attention focused on utility performance would be paralleled by equivalent oversight of the transportation community. Yet it is not.

In fairness to NYSDOT, the same criticisms could be leveled at most if not all states. The absence of any published statewide measures and the inability to provide comparative data with other states provides strong evidence of the imbalance of approaches between regulatory activities and state-provided services. A public transportation utility could be held to a level of performance responsive to the needs of society. It would be up to the transportation utility to determine when new roads are needed and to balance the cost of new construction against the costs of improved maintenance, management, and operations, thus disconnecting planning from the political process.

Definition of Public Utilities

A public utility (referred to here as a utility) is a company that maintains and/or operates the infrastructure for a public service. In this context, the infrastructure is considered the facilities and services needed for the functioning of an economy. It may be physical (roads, electrical distribution systems, water and sewer, etc.) or it may be organizational, including people and supporting facilities such as those found with the postal service.

Utilities may be either regulated or unregulated, monopolistic or competitive. Utilities offering a service whose associated infrastructure is expensive to replicate tend to be monopolistic. Monopolistic utilities are always regulated (by public service commissions or public utility commissions) to ensure that the best service is being provided at the lowest price. The degree of regulation tends to decrease or disappear as the level of competition increases. Electric, water, and sewer utilities tend to have the highest degree of regulation because the cost of their infrastructure precludes the introduction of competition. At the other end of the spectrum, parcel delivery services such as UPS and FedEx are largely unregulated because of the competitive environment in which they operate. In other words, competition breeds efficiency, which in turn reduces the need for regulation. In spite of the desirability of competition, the creation of a highway utility would have to be monopolistic since it would be impractical to consider the competitive introduction of parallel roadways serving the same origins and destinations, operated by competing firms. In the event that a highway utility is created, it would undoubtedly be heavily regulated.

Public utilities can either be publicly or privately owned. Publicly owned utilities are either created by a governmental entity (state, county or city) or are cooperatives that are owned by the customers they serve. Privately owned utilities are owned by their investors (stockholders). The ownership of the utility affects its performance, priorities, and customer service orientation. To be specific, an organization whose performance is judged based on its return on investment, and thus the satisfaction of their customers, will work hard to ensure that it is meeting its corporate responsibilities. In other words, performance and financial returns are directly related, as opposed to the existing upside down system of financial rewards. For this reason, the type of ownership defined for the utility is an important consideration, and private ownership is suggested.

The Transportation Utility

Imagine if the telephone system was operated in the same manner as the transportation system is currently managed. In some locations, there would be a long wait for a call to go through due to oversaturation. In other locations, the call would have a lot of static. In many locations, calls would be frequently interrupted with unpredictable time delays until their restoration. Callers would have no recourse since the telephone system would be operated by the government, which could not afford its expansion and modernization due to constrained tax revenue. It would also be unlikely that the telephone system would have adopted fiber optics communication, solid state switching, and sophisticated wireless communication. It would still be operating using 1960s technology since it would be funded by a government that avoided raising taxes and shunned innovative approaches to financing.

If you question this analogy, consider the fact that the 4,000 traffic signals in the city of Philadelphia are controlled using the electromechanical technology that was prevalent in the 1960s. This technology has not been updated in spite of the availability of modern solid state technology for the past thirty years. It goes without saying that the modern traffic signal controller is more reliable and requires less preventive maintenance than the earlier electromechanical controllers. **Philadelphia is experiencing a shortage of maintenance technicians required to repair this old technology – a problem that might have been relieved if this technology had been replaced with state-of-the-art equipment.** On the other hand, telephone companies throughout the United States have thrived as regulated utilities that benefit from technological developments—developments that have resulted in a highly innovative and competitive environment, which in turn has reduced the need for government regulation.

Assuming that you have been persuaded of the value of a transportation utility, what would it look like? It would be a monopolistic utility regulated by a public utilities commission (PUC). It would be privately owned and financed through stock offerings, and its income would be derived from a transportation utility fee assessed to all property owners within the jurisdictions it serves based on the traffic they generate. The creation of a utility offers many benefits including:

- Performance measurement—by its nature, the utility must collect measures as required by the PUC. If a nationwide network of utilities were to be created, performance measures would be standardized to facilitate comparison with other utilities.
- Attention to operations—the new public transportation utilities would be free of the construction legacy that burdens today's transportation agencies. They would be organized for efficient customer service in order to guarantee an acceptable rate of return to their investors.

All activities would be balanced against efficient use of existing infrastructure, since this is the way in which returns on investment would be maximized.

- Adoption of technology—it would be in the best interest of the transportation utility to use the latest applicable technology. Facilities would be updated as quickly as needed to ensure that their operating and maintenance costs do not exceed the value of investments in new technology. The artificial separation of capital costs and operating costs that exists within the transportation community would disappear.
- Human resources—the non-governmental nature of the transportation utility provides management with the ability to establish wages, employment policies, retirement programs, and career tracks needed to attract the individuals with the skills required for effective transportation M&O.
- Funding—subject to the oversight of the PUC, the transportation utility has the ability to issue stock and bonds required to finance new construction. It has the ability to establish rates required to ensure that high-quality transportation services are provided.
- Customer service—with its private sector culture, the transportation utility would by necessity prepare customer-oriented annual reports, automated call centers, and informative reports required to ensure the public's continued support.

Revenue Sources for the Transportation Utility

Potential revenue sources for the transportation system that have received the most attention these days are the gas tax, VMT pricing, and tolling; all of which have been discussed earlier. Interestingly, the concept of a utility fee has received little attention from the transportation community even though it has been successfully used by a number of communities and upheld by the courts. It is a fascinating approach to transportation financing, compatible with the concept of the transportation utility. Since a utility fee is considered a fee for service rather than a tax, it tends to escape the usual anti-tax political rhetoric. It offers an additional advantage over funding from income taxes or property taxes, in that everyone using the transportation system becomes a contributor. Tax-exempt organizations that utilize the transportation system must still pay for the service in much the same way that these organizations also pay their electric and water bills. Alternatively, those who purchase gasoline but do not use it for highway travel (boating, lawn mowing, etc.) would not be required to pay an inequitable tax. So there are many reasons to consider a utility fee as an alternative funding source for the nation's transportation system and one that provides the needed revenue source for the suggested transportation utility.

Transportation utility fees are described in detail by Reid Ewing in *Government Finance Review*.[85] They are based on the concept that every type of land use (residential, business, retail, etc.) must pay a fee related to the amount of traffic that they generate. Many communities rely on information published by the Institute of Transportation Engineers' (ITE) trip generation report,[86] which contains tables that define the number of trips generated for 162 types of land use. Just about every type of land use is included, as demonstrated by some of the newer additions to the report that include free-standing discount superstore, drive-in bank, and discount home furnishing superstore. These tables can be used to determine transportation utility fees on the assumption that the usage of the highway system is proportional to the number of trips that occur. Obviously, many would object to the use of these general numbers that benefit some and penalize others. For example, consider the elderly couple who live in their own residence and who do not own any vehicles. Should they be paying a transportation service fee? A similar question might be asked about school taxes, trash collection fees, and other municipal services that are charged based on the existence of a structure rather than the characteristics of its residents. In several cases, the courts have ruled that mathematical exactitude is not required as long as the fee is based on a defendable standard that is both equitable and repeatable.

It must be emphasized that the concept of a utility fee will be new to many jurisdictions. Its implementation may require new legislation in some states. It will also be subjected to numerous challenges by those who are currently receiving transportation services tax free, and those such as large shopping center owners whose taxes could be significant. However, the utility fee is an attractive alternative to actions such as an increased gasoline tax or the imposition of a VMT tax with its image of privacy violation and the requirement for major infrastructure investments.

Assuming the creation of a transportation utility, the process by which the utility fee is imposed would be similar to that by which electric utilities establish their rates. A rate is proposed by the utility based on its operating costs as well as its need for investment in new facilities and a reasonable return on its investment. The transportation utility commission staff would review the proposal for reasonableness, hold hearings, negotiate with the utility, and ultimately establish a rate. This is a time-tested proven process understood and accepted by both the public and the government regulators.

If nothing else, this discussion has demonstrated that the creation of a transportation utility is practical and an approach that offers significant benefits. But don't be fooled by the appeal of this approach. It represents an attack on traditional institutions, their employees, and the elected officials who benefit from their existence. A change of this magnitude is likely to be met with fierce opposition from those with an interest in the status quo.

The Evolution—Reinventing the DOT

If the thought of replacing existing public transportation agencies with a utility makes you uncomfortable, the alternative is to perform surgery on existing public agencies. If you were the surgeon, where would you begin your work?

During the past five or six years, Steve Lockwood, a well-known transportation management consultant, and I have been working on projects intended to move the state transportation agencies toward an increased emphasis on M&O. As a result of this work, a self-evaluation process has been developed that permits agencies to assess their performance in six dimensions.[87] These areas were carefully selected on the theory that a shortcoming in any one of the six dimensions would prevent acceptable levels of performance in the others. The process that evolved from this work is complex and won't be repeated here, except to identify the six critical dimensions that include:

- Business processes include the planning, financing, and evaluation activities that ensure agencies are taking a balanced approach to construction, management, and operations. In other words, are all relevant alternative actions to improving transportation services within a given region considered or is there an emphasis on new construction to the exclusion of all else?
- Systems and technology includes the use of the latest available technologies, applications of appropriate systems engineering tools, use of available standards, etc., appropriately applied?
- Performance measurement includes the degree to which an agency measures its performance and the manner in which this information is used (evaluation of ongoing activities, communicating with the public and elected officials, and setting goals for future performance).
- Culture has been discussed at length here. The appropriate culture is one in which there is a recognition of the fact that M&O must receive equal priority to new construction.
- Organization and workforce includes the structure of the organization and the degree of visibility given to M&O activities. (i.e., at what level of the organization is it assigned?) This category also addresses the processes used for recruitment, promotion, training, and retention of key staff members.
- Collaboration is an important consideration for the transportation agencies. Cooperative relationships must exist with adjacent political jurisdictions, local governments, public safety agencies, planning organizations, and private sector organizations such as towing companies.

Since developing the self-improvement process, Steve and I have met with a number of transportation agencies throughout the United States with the objective of identifying their strengths and weaknesses for the purpose of developing an agency improvement program. The results of these meetings have been instructive. Attendees have actively participated in the process and offered frank assessments of their agency's performance. Yet when the self-improvement plan was discussed, there was resistance to defining the needed actions to strengthen their operation for a variety of reasons, including lack of management support, inadequate resources to implement the changes, and failure to appreciate the importance of performance measurement and customer service.

The lesson learned from these experiences is that change within a public agency comes very slowly and may only occur following a catastrophic event such as the Valentine's Day ice storm experienced in Pennsylvania during which motorists were trapped in their cars for nearly a day. For this reason, evolutionary change beyond minor adjustments is needed. The change must be significant, justified, and supported by the most senior leaders of the agency as well as by the elected officials who control its destiny. The change must be capable of demonstrating noticeable benefits that will win the public support, which determines the attitudes of these officials.

The Constituents of Change

The list of six critical dimensions is not unique. It could be applied to health care, law enforcement, and telecommunications, as readily as it is applied to transportation. Similarly, the actions required to strengthen the entire suite of dimensions are not unique. They include organizational modification such that all of its functions receive equal attention, freeing funding from the artificial constraints of the political and legislative process, improving staff strength in both numbers and skills, and creating a climate that encourages technological risk-taking. Some of these actions, such as the reorganization of the enterprise, can be taken without requiring legislative approval. Others such as modifications to the political process require the approval of higher authorities.

Organizational modification (a.k.a. reorganization) is at the heart of the suggested changes. Because no two DOTs are the same and they all differ from their city and county counterparts, it is difficult to provide more than guiding principles for a reorganization of this nature. First and foremost, the DOTs primary activities of planning, roadway projects (including design and construction), bridges, maintenance, safety, traffic engineering, and M&O should all be reporting to the chief executive officer of the agency at an equal level. This is a change from today's organization in which M&O is typically assigned four or five levels down from the office of the chief executive (secretary of transportation or administrator). There are likely to be many variations; for example, some agencies might also include an environmental office at the same level. Others might elect to combine the M&O activity with the safety activity. But the key change is that of elevating the office of M&O such that it is of equal importance to the other activities within the organization. In addition, all M&O activities should be contained within a single department or office. Many state departments of transportation feel that their primary responsibility is freeway operation. They assign arterial operations a lower level of importance, failing to recognize that the arterials in most states carry more than one-half of the traffic flow. The integration of the two into a single office will ensure that they receive equal attention.

The second guiding principle for the reorganization is that the planning activity (typically known as the office of planning or the planning department) should be assigned the function of trading off construction with additional M&O activities. For example, when the possibility of an additional freeway lane is being considered, the planning office must be required to compare this construction against the use of shoulder lanes during peak periods, the use of ramp metering, and the use of expanded incident management. When appropriate, the analysis should also consider the possibility of other enhancements to the corridor being served by the freeway, such as improved signal timing and expanded transit service on parallel routes. In other words, this new planning activity should be responsible for comparing the benefits of M&O and transit with the possibility of new construction. The next step of the process is the translation of the results of the analysis into a funding plan, which would treat funding for appropriate M&O actions in the same manner as funding identified for construction. These steps are often ignored during the planning process, although it is not a new concept for some of the more progressive DOTs. The new planning activity must be further expanded to include the outreach needed to convince elected officials that a plan, which may not necessarily include new visible construction, is to be preferred over the investments in new roadways. It is the responsibility of this activity to collect needed performance measures and to use these measures as the basis to fight for a balanced approach to transportation.

While reorganization is generally possible without requiring extensive external participation, the development of a talented, well-educated, and proactive staff open to the use of leading edge technology is more difficult to accomplish without legislative and sometimes union backing. This type of support is required because it involves changing position descriptions, increasing salaries, enhancing training programs, and a myriad of other forms of compensation that are usually spelled out by the governmental entity within which the agency resides. Existing restrictive policies eliminate the agility required by a high-tech organization of the type required to develop the twenty-first-century highway system. Thus, while organizational issues are readily defined and accomplished, personnel and technology issues require a different approach—outsourcing.

Outsourcing

Outsourcing is defined as the act of contracting for provision of a business function that used to be performed in-house. There are many examples of outsourcing. For example, during a recent hospital stay, I learned that all meals were provided by Sodexo Health Care Services, a worldwide food service company. In essence, the hospital had outsourced its food services to Sodexo to the great benefit and appreciation of the patients. Similarly today's transportation agencies routinely outsource functions such as freeway service patrols, staffing of traffic management centers, grass mowing and landscaping, maintenance, and paving. Specialized functions such as high tech system design and implementation are routinely outsourced to consultants and systems integrators.

Wikipedia lists eighteen reasons for outsourcing, many of which are applicable to the transportation community.[88] Some of the more compelling reasons from the perspective of the reinvented DOT include:

- Cost restructuring—operating leverage is a measure that compares fixed costs to variable costs. Outsourcing changes the balance of this ratio by offering a move from the fixed cost of a permanent staff to the variable cost of staffing and equipment that can be allocated to an activity on an as-needed basis.
- Improve quality—improved quality can be achieved through incentive-based contracting in which contractor fees and profits are tied to the quality of service provided.
- Knowledge—contracted services may provide an agency with access to intellectual property and staff specialties that are not available within the agency itself.
- Contract—services are provided according to the terms of a binding contract with financial penalties and legal redress.
- Access to talent—access to a larger talent pool and a sustainable source of skills, in particular in science and engineering.
- Catalyst for change—an organization can use an outsourcing agreement as a catalyst for major step change that cannot be achieved alone.
- Enhance capacity for innovation—companies increasingly use external knowledge service providers to supplement limited in-house capacity for product innovation.

While there are many advantages to outsourcing, it would be naive to ignore its drawbacks. Many of those in the public sector with outsourcing experience have expressed concern that outsourced services increase the cost of delivering these services when the cost of public sector oversight of the outsourced activities is taken into account. Depending on the nature of the services, they also complain that contractors often assign personnel to a project that are unfamiliar with the unique aspects of the roadways for which they are responsible. For example, an outsourced emergency service patrol operator may not know the local roads and may not be acquainted with police and fire personnel with whom he must work. These significant issues must be addressed during the outsourcing process. It is possible, even likely, that these disadvantages can be minimized through the issuance of a long duration contract with a broad range of responsibilities that provides the outsource contractor with the ability to develop a stable and trained staff. It may be possible to minimize the overhead costs of contract management through the use of a contract scope that utilizes a single contractor to provide a broader range of services, thus spreading the management costs over a larger base.

What to Outsource

There is little doubt that outsourcing of government services is here to stay. The challenge to the transportation sector is identification of the suite of services as candidates for outsourcing that will result in a net benefit to the agency. While a detailed analysis of the functions of a DOT is beyond the scope of the book, there are several interesting possibilities. First is the possibility of geographic outsourcing. What if an agency were to outsource all of the management, operations, maintenance, and construction of an entire roadway or of a major transportation corridor? The selected contractor would be responsible for all services associated with the corridor, including maintenance, landscaping, drainage, lighting, traffic signals, signs, and pavement markings. The contract under which the work is performed would be a performance-based contract in which the contractor would be rewarded for the ride quality, aesthetic appearance, safety record, and travel time and delays that existed within the roadway or corridor. Performance adjustments would be made in the event that new development, such as the construction of a shopping center, were to occur that had an impact on any of these criteria. In short, the contractor would become the operator of the roadway or corridor. The contract would not be prescriptive, in the sense that it would not define requirements for frequency of maintenance activities, times at which signal timing is to be updated, or number of service patrol vehicles required. It would be up to the contractor to determine the manner in which these functions would be performed.

The second alternative form of outsourcing is functional outsourcing. What if an agency outsourced an entire traffic signal system, including its maintenance, equipment replacement and upgrades, and operation? Like the geographic outsourcing, this alternative would be implemented using a performance-based contract. Performance criteria might include response times to replace a burned out bulb or to fix an intersection that was damaged as the result of an accident. It would also include measurement of travel times and delays impacted by the signal system. It would be up to the contractor to determine the appropriate times to replace aging equipment based on a calculation of the cost of maintaining the equipment versus the cost of its replacement. These actions should be performed by any well-managed organization, except that the public sector is constrained from capital improvements by an archaic funding system. If it works, don't replace it. Remember the Philadelphia example?

Both the geographic and functional outsourcing described here exceed most forms of outsourcing currently in use. Their sweeping scope offers the potential for overcoming the shortcomings described above—that is, management costs and lack of familiarity. Performance-based outsourcing forces contractors to become intimately familiar with the transportation needs of the region they serve. The planning activity described above becomes an implicit feature of this type of outsourcing since the contractor would be continuously performing trade-offs between investment in maintenance versus replacement.

It would be remiss to ignore the impact of outsourcing on existing agency staff. In outsourcing situations, it is common for the contractor to hire existing agency staff possessing the skills required to meet the contract requirements. Staff members making the transition from the public to the private sector are typically employed for an evaluation period of somewhere between ninety days and six months. Depending upon their performance, staff members would be retained by the outsource contractor.

Moving Forward

The purpose of this discussion is to persuade you, the reader, that we are not stuck with our existing twentieth-century roadway system. In order to move toward the twenty-first-century highway system, significant changes will be required. If you remember Chapter 1 of this book, you will recognize that the existing structure of state DOTs, accompanied by significant federal oversight, has only been in existence for the past fifty years. It is time to consider new structures that rely increasingly on the private sector for their success.

No matter which alternative is selected, the challenge faced by the public sector, including both its agencies and elected officials, is not to over-regulate. After all, one of the reasons for the failure of private toll roads during the nineteenth century was excessive government regulation. A recent article in the *Washington Post* epitomizes the over-regulation syndrome.[89] This article describes a plan introduced by the chairman of the Washington, DC city council that proposes that 51 percent of all new employees hired by contractors who work on city contracts be District residents. While the motivation of a rule like this is well meaning, it has the effect of negating the benefits offered by private sector participation. It eliminates the flexibility of assigning the best employees to a given project and prevents introducing specialized skills that may be required. But this is just one of many examples of the manner in which the meddling of the political system can destroy a worthwhile concept.

Another challenge is to find the political will at both the federal and state levels to experiment with new forms of roadway management and to abandon the pork barrel that the highway trust fund has come to represent. Unless this occurs, we are stuck with a decaying twentieth-century highway system, to the detriment of the nation's economy and society in general.

CHAPTER 12

Going Forward

What the caterpillar calls the end of the world,
the master calls a butterfly.

—Richard Bach[90]

Where Do We Go From Here?

On September 10, 2009, the Miller Center for Public Affairs at the University of Virginia sponsored a bipartisan conference led by former secretaries of transportation Norman Mineta and Samuel Skinner to "facilitate, at a critical time, original and necessary thinking about the financing, governance and management of America's transportation infrastructure."[91] The opening statement from this conference accurately captures the issues associated with our twentieth-century transportation system when it states that:

A system launched with a bold and historic vision half a century ago is now characterized by pork and political opportunism. Financing models that once served America well are no longer sustainable. Stimulus funding will add capacity in some communities and will bring other elements of the system into a state of better repair, but will not provide the efficient, scalable, state-of-the-art transportation system necessary to drive future economic growth. What's needed is nothing less than a fundamental overhaul of America's transportation policies and programs.

These thoughts are not unique. In 2005, Congress created the National Surface Transportation Policy and Revenue Study Commission. This high-level commission was made up of twelve members representing federal, state, and local governments; metropolitan planning organizations; transportation-related industries; and public interest organizations. Its purpose was to examine the current condition and future needs of the nation's transportation system as well as alternatives to the fuel tax as a principle revenue source. The commission's work was completed in 2008.[92] In its final report, it too captures the importance of the transportation system to the American economy and quality of life in the following succinct statement:

"Our families and firms can no longer tolerate excessive transportation constraints that waste our collective resources—time, money, fuel, clean air, and our competitive edge."[93]

Thus, the nation's leadership collectively recognizes that our transportation system, which is the lifeblood of our economy, badly needs an overhaul. Our quality of life and national well-being rely on its continued effectiveness. Yet the recommendations of these two commissions as well as others offer solutions that do little more than fine-tune existing processes, strengthen weak areas, and uniformly push for significant increases in funding. In other words, they are working around the edges trying to make a failed system work. Bold new approaches such as the ones proposed in the previous chapter are required. And yet they are not suggested. In fact, there is no evidence that they were even considered.

The plan described in this chapter, which builds on the concepts discussed earlier, addresses the need for a fundamental overhaul. All that is required is the national will to pursue an approach that differs from business as usual.

A Framework for Change

The terrorist attacks of September 11, 2001 proved to be an extreme test of our society. There were acts of bravery, terror, and mind-numbing sorrow on that day. But there was also a test of the emergency response systems in the two cities affected by these tragic events, with both positive and negative results. In the Washington, DC region, the lack of coordination among emergency responders and information sources was particularly troubling. This should not have been terribly surprising given that there are more than twenty-four law enforcement agencies within the Washington, DC region. Within the District of Columbia alone, these agencies include the Metropolitan Police Department, the District of Columbia Protective Services Police, the Metro Transit Police, the U.S. Park Police, the U.S. Capitol Police, the Secret Service, the National Zoo Police, the U.S. Mint Police, the Federal Protective Service, and the State Department Police. It is not surprising that the response to a major incident such as that of September 11 would be chaotic at best.

From the public's perspective, the most concrete evidence of the chaos was the information they received, which was sometimes conflicting and often non-existent. For example, the Metropolitan Police Department ordered the Washington Metropolitan Area Transit Administration (WMATA) to shut down the subway system, an order that was refused, with the results that the trains kept running. Some of the media reported that the system had been shut down, and others reported that it was still in operation. There was also an order to evacuate the city, an order that was complicated by the fact that the bridges between DC and Virginia had been closed to all traffic. Here again, conflicting media reports aggravated the situation.

In the aftermath of the crisis, the Greater Washington Board of Trade, a network of the region's business leaders, requested the creation of an information outlet that would serve as a consolidated, reliable source of information regarding the status of the transportation system in the DC region. I attended the initial meeting with the Board of Trade, at which their request was made, in support of the Maryland State Highway Administration. The meeting occurred in the spring of 2003. On the surface, it would seem to be a simple task to form an organization whose mission is to provide the DC region with information related to the status of its transportation systems. After all, there are precedents for this type of organization in other parts of the country, such as the TRANSCOM organization that serves the greater New York City metropolitan area. However, the task of coordinating two states (Maryland and Virginia) and the District of Columbia, along with multiple cities and counties, proved to be formidable. There were many meetings among the representatives of the regional transportation agencies to discuss the scope and responsibilities of the new organization and, more importantly, the manner in which it would be funded. There were presentations to the regional transportation planning board that oversees transportation issues of regional interest, committees were formed, reports were written, and finally on July 1, 2009, the Metropolitan Area Transportation Operations Coordination (MATOC) program was established.

The point of this anecdote is that six years were required for the creation of a new organization with the relatively narrow mission of providing situational awareness for a regional transportation system. Imagine the time that might be required to restructure a major system of existing agencies that exist within a political system benefiting from their existence. MATOC was formed in response to a crisis situation that had demonstrated the need for such an organization. Yet it took six years. There is no equally compelling event on which to base the restructuring of the manner in which our twentieth-century highway system is currently operated. It can be left to gradually deteriorate at a slow pace that will permit those who are currently responsible for its present condition to blame the situation on their predecessors. Those who have spent their careers in a system where decades might be required for the realization of a new roadway have lost their sense of urgency. They are accustomed to waiting for long periods of time to accomplish their goals.

But we can't wait that long. A number of changes have been recommended in the preceding chapters and some of these changes can be readily implemented, and, in fact, some of the recommended changes are already underway. The revolutionary change proposed for the state DOTs is more difficult and will require many years for its successful implementation.

As a result, a plan has been structured that is organized into both short-term and-long term actions. Both the evolutionary changes and the revolutionary changes have been incorporated in this plan since they are not mutually exclusive.

Short-term Actions

Workforce Development

Top among the list of short-term actions is the issue of workforce development. It does no good to restructure a system that is incapable of acquiring adequate personnel to meet its objectives. Implicit in the Chapter 9 discussion of workforce development is the need for leadership and specific actions by the USDOT. The federal government should prepare a workforce development plan that identifies the actions and resources needed to attract and train individuals to acquire the skills needed across the board for the management and operation of the twenty-first-century highway system. The plan should include recommendations regarding position descriptions and salary levels. It should also address possible approaches to relieving the immediate problem of workforce inadequacies through outsourcing, employment of consultants, and the use of universities.

At the same time, the USDOT should begin a proactive program to encourage and support the development of certificate programs for universities with relevant academic curricula. Here again, this is a relatively straightforward activity that could be underway in less than a year from the decision to proceed.

These actions are readily accomplished at a very low cost. The workforce development plan should be accompanied with a cost estimate for the implementation of the plan. In fact, at the time of this writing in early 2011, I became aware of a just such a development. The USDOT ITS Joint Program Office (JPO) is nearing the completion of a plan that addresses some of these issues. The plan in its current draft form emphasizes the training and educational aspects of workforce development. However, it fails to address the issue of attracting more individuals to the profession, as well as the issues of salary and career paths for existing employees. But on a positive note, the existence of the plan further supports the recommendations made in Chapter 9, as well as the idea that these recommendations can be implemented as a short-term action. Clearly, more work needs to be done.

Technology

A recent article in the *Washington Post* neatly captured the need for establishing an improved bridge between innovation and adoption of technology by the transportation community when it quoted Charles Weiss, a Georgetown University professor specializing in innovation. "Go to American universities, and you'll see people are brimming with great ideas." The *Post* adds, "The problem: Grand new ideas where we need them most—in energy, transportation and health care—bang up against the old ways of doing things."[94] The introduction of innovative technology requires that the old ways of doing things be abandoned in favor of new processes that encourage and streamline the adoption of the great ideas being developed in the universities and corporations throughout the United States.

Chapter 10 addresses various approaches for accelerating the introduction and use of technology by the surface transportation community. As indicated in this chapter, public sector agency staff members recognize the need for advanced technology but are prevented from taking advantage of its benefits due to institutional constraints. This chapter suggests that the use of technology can best be accelerated through a series of innovative programs that encourage industry participation in the form of collaborative responsibility and ownership of various public facilities in projects that offer a revenue-producing potential— in other words, P3s built around the use of new technology. As indicated in Chapter 10, this approach differs significantly from the traditional government-led approach in which the government comes up with the *good ideas*, and industry competes for their implementation.

Traditionally, the FHWA has approached trials of unique technologies and partnerships by funding field operational tests (FOTs). FOTs are essentially projects intended to demonstrate the value of the technologies being tested. The FOTs require the selection of a volunteer agency (the owner of the highway system), the competitive selection of a contractor to implement the test, and the selection of a firm given the responsibility to evaluate the test results. This tends to be an arduous process during which several years are needed to complete the selection and contracting to support the tests, followed by two or three years to complete the work and evaluate the results. Thus, the relatively simple process of testing and evaluating a specific technology may require five or more years for its completion. Only then would it be ready for prime time, which means that the process of persuading other agencies of its value then begins. Is it any wonder that more than fifteen years are needed for new technologies to see the light of day within the highway community?

For this reason, a more streamlined approach is needed. One approach worth considering is used by VDOT, which takes an aggressive approach to both outsourcing and P3s. The approach used has been so successful that as of 2006, nearly 60 percent of VDOTs budget was expended on private vendors.[95] VDOT advertises its interest and willingness to accept private sector partners and encourages interested parties to submit proposals in a variety of areas related to the construction, maintenance, management, and operation of the state's transportation system. Proposals are evaluated by a committee in terms of their benefits to the Commonwealth (Virginia is a commonwealth rather than a state) and a number of other well-defined criteria. Contracts are then negotiated with the successful offerers. Depending on the size and complexity of the project, this process can be completed within a year.

VDOT further encourages P3s and other initiatives through the creation of a Transportation Partnership Opportunity Fund.[96] The fund's total resources of $50 million are allocated by the governor for a maximum project size of $5 million. Money can be distributed in the form of grants, revolving loans, or equity contributions to an agency, a political subdivision, or a private organization that has submitted a proposal or signed an agreement for the development of a transportation facility in Virginia.

Public-private partnerships are not unique. In fact, the FHWA has published a manual that includes examples and model legislation to be used in states that do not currently permit this type of activity.[97] However, almost without exception, the examples provided in the FHWA report include the construction of roads, toll facilities, and bridges. No P3s related to the introduction of new technology are described. This shortcoming is further evidence of the construction mentality that exists at both the state and federal levels.

The plan to accelerate the implementation of new technology should be based on the development of P3s in which the public sector and the private sector, or universities, can offer technology-based concepts to be implemented on the nation's roadways using P3 arrangements. The plan should be managed by the USDOT (either FHWA or the JPO), which would assume responsibility for advertising its existence, distributing funding (as needed), and reviewing all proposals. All submissions should be based on a partnership between a public sector owner and either the private sector or a university. All submissions must be based on the introduction of a new technology, which will be demonstrated in a manner that offers the promise to become self-sustaining.

The program for the acceleration of new technology should be accompanied by a special fund, similar to VDOT's Transportation Partnership Opportunity Fund, that offers seed money and other resources to encourage creative thinking, partnerships, and proposals needed to ensure the success of the program. Only modest funding would be required since some of the needed resources would be derived from the proposal partners, and some of the funding could be in the form of loans and loan guarantees.

The success of this program should be judged based on the accelerated introduction and use of new technologies. Successes should be tracked, recorded, and disseminated throughout the transportation community. Both the technology and the process by which it was developed and implemented should be included in the outreach. To the extent permitted by law, the traditional constraints on procurement of new technologies should be avoided, such as the need to ensure a competitive selection, preferences based on corporate ownership (minorities, women, veterans, etc.), and government audits of overhead and other intrusive measures.

A streamlined program, enhanced by seed funding, and without unnecessary restrictions offers the potential to uncover, test, and demonstrate those great ideas highlighted in the *Washington Post* article. Assuming its success, this program will also provide ideas and guidance related to the rapid adoption of new technology by the transportation community.

Organization

Workforce and technology changes are easy when compared to the organizational changes described in Chapter 11, which suggests both evolutionary and revolutionary changes. These two types of changes are not mutually exclusive but can be pursued in parallel.

The evolutionary change is a modest incremental fine-tuning of DOT organizations. As you may recall, it suggested consolidating and increasing the organizational status of the M&O activity and creating a planning organization that increasingly emphasizes M&O and expands its outsourcing activities. However, in spite of their obvious benefits, DOTs have been slow to embrace the principles described. Increased emphasis needs to be place on this aspect of the needed organizational changes through education, publication, and encouragement of these public agencies. The responsibility for this activity falls on FHWA, which is already encouraging the planning and outsourcing activities that have been described. This is clearly a near-term activity. FHWA should expand these activities to include recommendations related to the disposition of the M&O activity.

On the other hand, the creation of the transportation utility is a much longer-term activity. Planning for this radical change to the structure of the public transportation agencies should begin immediately. Changes of this nature require extensive preliminary preparation, including employment of outside consultants to define the details of the concept, identify the potential legal obstacles, and perform the hard work of justifying its viability. The preparation for a change of this nature is a multi-year activity that will entail extensive discussion and debate prior to its implementation. Due to the significance and complexity of this activity, the initial preparatory steps should be initiated immediately.

Long-term Actions

Not too much can be said about the long-term actions, except that the concept of the transportation utility is further developed within this time frame. Undoubtedly, it includes the passage of legislation at both federal and state levels as required to legalize the concept. In addition, it requires legislation that supports the transportation utility fee described in Chapter 11.

Since much of this legislation must be introduced on a state-by-state basis, it is suggested that a candidate DOT be identified for a proof of concept demonstration. Either a small state (Rhode Island?) or a portion of a larger state (a district or region) should be considered for the proof of concept. The region should consider a metropolitan area that includes some congested roadways and a variety of facilities. The test must be realistic if it is to be accepted by other agencies observing its results. The details of these long-term actions would be determined by the consulting study conducted as a short-term activity.

During the time period beyond the short-term actions, continuing attention must be placed on the workforce development and technology improvements that have been discussed. If a transportation utility is to be successful, ideally it should be based on the shoulders of a competent workforce using appropriate advanced technologies to ensure its effectiveness.

But with that, I am certain that you, the reader, are happy to learn that the discussion of next steps is drawing to a close with the details of their implementation being left to others.

Final Thoughts

Writing a book of this nature is very challenging. In addition to describing the current situation persuasively and identifying feasible solutions to an extremely difficult problem, it is necessary to present this material in a suitably entertaining manner to keep the readers awake. If you are reading this closing paragraph, I have succeeded. If you are persuaded by the arguments presented, I am ecstatic. Hopefully, this book will lead to a groundswell for improved transportation services and more effective use of a scarce resource—tax dollars. The transportation system is too critical to the country's economic health and the quality of life for its residents to allow the current rate of decay to continue.

Acronyms

AASHTO—American Association of State Highway and Transportation Officials

ABS—Automatic Breaking Systems

AHS—Automated Highway System

ASAI—Average Service Availability Index

ASCE—American Society of Civil Engineers

BAC—Blood Alcohol Concentration

BPR—Bureau of Public Roads

CAIDI—Customer Average Interruption Duration Index for electric utilities

Caltrans—California Department of Transportation

CCTV—Closed Circuit Television

CDOT—Colorado Department of Transportation

CE—Civil Engineering

CLRP—Constrained Long Range Plan

DALY—Disability Adjusted Life Year

DC—District of Columbia (shorthand for Washington, DC)

DMS—Dynamic Message Signs

DOT—Department of Transportation

DSRC—Dedicated Short Range Communication

DUI—Driving Under the Influence (of alcohol)

DWI – Driving While Intoxicated

EA—Environmental Assessment

EIS—Environmental Impact Statement

FedEx—Federal Express

FHWA—Federal Highway Administration (a unit of the U.S. Department of Transportation)

FOT—Field Operational Test

FTMC—First Transcontinental Motor Convoy

HOT—High Occupancy Toll lanes

HOV—High Occupancy Vehicle lanes

ICC—Intercounty Connector

ISP—Information Services Provider

IT—Information Technology

ITE—Institute of Transportation Engineers

ITS—Intelligent Transportation Systems

JIT—Just in Time (delivery)

JPO—Joint Program Office

KDOT—Kansas Department of Transportation

LRTP—Long Range Transportation Plan

M&O—Management and Operations

MADD—Mothers Against Drunk Driving

Metropolitan Area Transportation Operations Coordination

MIPS—Maryland Industrial Partners program

Mn/DOT—Minnesota Department of Transportation

MoDOT—Missouri Department of Transportation

MPO—Metropolitan Planning Organization

NCHRP—National Cooperative Highway Research Program

NEPA—National Environmental Policy Act

NHTSA—National Highway Traffic Safety Administration

NYSDOT—New York State Department of Transportation

OBU—Onboard Unit of the VII program

OPEC—Organization of Petroleum Exporting Countries

P3—Public Private Partnership

PANY—Port Authority of New York

PB—Parsons Brinckerhoff Inc.

PennDOT—Pennsylvania Department of Transportation

PEPCO—Potomac Electric Power Company

PMT—Person Miles of Travel

PSC—Public Service Commission (used in conjunction with the New York State PSC)

PUC—Public Utilities Commission

RIDOT—Rhode Island Department of Transportation

RITA—Research and Innovative Technology Administration of the USDOT

RSU—Roadside Unit of the VII program

SAIDI—System Average Interruption Duration Index for electric utilities

SAIFI—System Average Interruption Frequency Index for electric utilities

SBIR—Small Business Innovative Research program

SCOOT—The acronym has been created using the traffic signal timing terminology as follows: Split Cycle Offset Optimization Technique. It refers to an automated form of traffic signal control in which the timing is automatically adjusted for current traffic patterns.

SSOM—Subcommittee on System Operations and Management

STIP—Statewide Transportation Improvement Plan

TBTA—Triborough Bridge and Tunnel Authority

TIP—Transportation Improvement Plan

TOC—Traffic Operations Center

TTI—Texas Transportation Institute

UAV—Unmanned Aerial Vehicle

UPS—United Parcel Service

USPS—United States Postal Service

VDOT—Virginia Department of Transportation

VII—Vehicle Infrastructure Integration

VMS—Variable Message Signs
VMT—Vehicle Miles of Travel
WHO—World Health Organization
WMATA—Washington Metropolitan Transit Administration

Notes

1. Dr. Joseph Sussman, "ITS Then and Now," *Civil Engineering*, March 2004.
2. Steven Wright, as cited by *Brainy Quote*, http://www.brainyquote.com/quotes/authors/s/steven_wright.html.
3. "The Braddock Expedition of 1755: Catastrophe in the Wilderness," *Historical Society of Pennsylvania*, 1, http//www.hsp.org/default.aspx?id-622.
4. "The Braddock Expedition: Battle of the Monongahela," *Wikipedia*, http://en.wsikipedia.org/wiki/Braddock_expedition.
5. Ibid.
6. George Washington, "Braddock's Defeat," a letter written by 23-year-old George Washington to his mother, Mary Washington, July 18, 1755, http://www.nationalcenter.org/Braddock'sDefeat.html.
7. The popular theory that Braddock's defeat resulted from the time-honored European tactics of ranks of troops opening fire using mass volleys as opposed to the Indian style skirmish tactics is still being debated. It is significant that Washington's letter to his mother disputes this theory when he says that "In short, the dastardly behavior of those they call regulars exposed all others, that were inclined to do their duty, to almost certain death; and, at last, in despite of all the efforts of the officers to the contrary, they ran, as sheep pursued by dogs, and it was impossible to rally them." Ibid 5. But the debate over tactics of warfare is beyond the scope of this book.
8. "Art and Paintings of the Revolutionary War," D.W. Roth, http://www.dwroth.com/bissell.htm#back.
9. "The Long Riders Guild Academic Foundation--The Tremendous Ride of Post Rider Israel Bissell," http://www.lrgaf.org/journeys/bissell.htm.
10. "Connecticut Roads," Kurumi, http://www.kurumi.com/roads/ct/us1.html.
11. "California--Trails and Roads: El Camino Real," www.cahighways.org.
12. "Stagecoach," http://en.wikipedia.org/wiki/Stagecoach.
13. Mary A. Helmich, "A Moving Experience by Stage," *Interpretation and Education Division*, California State Parks, 2008.
14. Elizabeth C. MacPhail, "Wells Fargo in San Diego," *The Journal of San Diego History* 28, no. 4 (1980).
15. Daniel Klein and John Majewski, "Turnpikes and Toll Roads in Nineteenth Century America," February 2010, http://eh.net/encyclopedia/article/klein.majewski.turnpikes.

176

16. Plank roads were constructed using two parallel rows of timbers four to five feet apart that were used as the foundation for the road. Eight-foot planks, three to four inches thick were then laid across the timbers. The planks were only secured by their own weight. Daniel Klein and John Majewski, "Plank Road Fever in Antebellum America: New York State Origins," *New York History*, 1994, 42-43.

17. "President Dwight Eisenhower and America's Interstate System," *Historynet.com*, http://www.historynet.com/president-dwight-eisenhower-and-americas-interstate-highway-system.htm.

18. Ibid.

19. "Interstate Frequently Asked Questions," FHWA, USDOT website, http://www.fhwa.dot.gov/interstate/faq.htm#question.

20. "The Numbers Game: How it Works with the Interstate System, FHWA News," June 1981, http://www.interstate50th.org/FHWAstats.pdf.

21. AASHO was subsequently renamed the American Association of State Highway and Transportation Officials (AASHTO).

22. Norman Mineta, "National Strategy to Reduce Congestion on America's Transportation Network," *USDOT*, May 2006, http://isddc.dot.gov/OLPFiles/OST/012988.pdf.

23. "Commuters Suffer Extreme Stress," *BBC News*, November 2004, http://news.bbc.co.uk/2/hi/uk_news/4052861.stm.

24. "Second Quarter 2009--Sales Up 2.2%," *The Capella University Online*, August 17, 2009, http://ecommerce.suite101.com/article.cfm/second_quarter_2009_online_sales_up_22.

25. Alternburg, et al., "Just-In-Time Logistics Support for the Automobile Industry," *Bloomfield State College*, Bloomfield, NJ, http://www.sole.or.kr/%EB%AC%BC%EB%A5%98%EC%86%8C%EC%8B%9D/JUST-IN-TIME%20LOGISTICS%20SUPPORT%20FOR%twentiethE%20AUTOMOBILE%20INDUSTRY.pdf.

26. "Traffic Nightmares Beginning to Cost Cities," *USA Today*, June 2010, http://www.usatoday.com/news/nation/2002-10-17-traffic_x.htm.

27. "Growing Traffic Congestion Threatens Nation's Economy, Quality of Life--Policy and Legislation--Address by Federal Highway Administrator Mary E. Peters--Brief Article," *Public Roads*, July-August 2002, http://findarticles.com/p/articles/mi_m3724/is_1_66/ai_91719278/.

28. Keith Glessen, "Letter From Moscow--Stuck, The Meaning of the City's Traffic Nightmare," *The New Yorker*, August 2, 2010, 24-28.

29. Vladimir Sorokin, *The Queue* (New York: Readers International, 1955). ISBN 978-I-59017-274-2.

30. Charles Kuralt, *On the Road With Charles Kuralt*, as cited by Welcome to the Quote Garden, http://www.quotegarden.com/travel.html.

31. David Schrank and Tim Lomax, "2009 Urban Mobility Report," *Texas Transportation Institute*, College Station Texas, 2010, http://mobility.tamu.edu/ums/report/.

32. "Beltway Burden: The Combined Cost of Housing and Transportation in the Washington, DC Metropolitan Area," *Urban Land Institute*, Washington, DC, 2009. http://commerce.uli.org/misc/BeltwayBurden.pdf.
33. "Beltway Burden: The Combined Cost of Transportation and Housing in the Greater Washington, DC Metropolitan Area," *Urban Land Institute*, Maryland, 2009.
34. "New Bridge Monitoring Devices Go Unused," *USA Today*, August 7, 2007, 1.
35. "Federal-Aid Program Administration," Highway Planning and Project Development Process--Memos, US Department of Transportation, *Federal Highway Administration*, http://www.fhwa.dot.gov/programadmin/mega/process.cfm.
36. Bill Cosby, quote from *Brainy Quote*, http://www.brainyquote.com/quotes/authors/b/bill_cosby.html.
37. "World Report on Road Traffic Injury Prevention: Summary," *World Health Organization*, Geneva 2004.
38. "Halving Roadway Fatalities," International Technology Scanning Program, sponsored by the US Department of Transportation, Federal Highway Administration, April 2006. http://international.fhwa.dot.gov/halving_fatalities/.
39. Ibid, 5.
40. Ibid, 17.
41. "Traffic Safety Facts, 2005 Data," *NHTSA National Center for Statistics and Analysis*, Washington, DC, DOT HS 810 629 (speed) and DOT HS 810 616 (alcohol).
42. "About: Alcoholism & Substance Abuse," http://alcoholism.about.com/.
43. DUI.COM, http://www.dui.com/states/california/dui_library/dui_countermeasures.html.
44. "Ignition Interlock--Issue Brief," *MADD Online*, http://www.madd.org/activism/0,1056,7604,00.html.
45. "Federal Highway Administration 1998 National Strategic Plan," http://www.fhwa.dot.gov/policy/fhplan.html#safety.
46. "Halving Roadway Fatalities," 12.
47. Werner Finck, quote from the *Quote Garden*, http://www.quotegarden.com/government.
48. "National Traffic Signal Report Card--Technical Report: 2007," US Department of Transportation, *Federal Highway Administration*, October 2007, 22.
49. "List of Countries by Traffic-Related Death Rate for Year 2000," *Wikipedia*, http://en.wikipedia.org/wiki/List_of_countries_by_traffic-related_death_rate.
50. Jonathan Serrie, "State DOTs: A Word From Our Sponsor," *FOX News Live Shots*, October 4, 2010, http://liveshots.blogs.foxnews.com/2010/10/04/state-dots-a-word-from-our-sponsor/#ixzz11PokxhSe.

51. "Rate of Return from Highway Investment," *National Cooperative Highway Research Program (NCHRP)*, no. 20-24(28), submitted by Delcan Inc., August 2005.

52. "Report Card for America's Infrastructure," *American Society of Civil Engineers*, 2005, http://apps.asce.org/reportcard/2005/page.cfm?id=30.

53. Wilson, Harold, quote from *Brainy Quote*, http://www.brainyquote.com/quotes/authors/h/harold_wilson.html.

54. "Kansas Department of Transportation 2009 Annual Report, Secretary's Message," http://www.ksdot.org/PDF_Files/KDOTReport-09FINAL.pdf.

55. Philip Tarnoff, "State of the Practice in Signal Timing Practices and Procedures," prepared for the *Institute of Transportation Engineers*, March 2004.

56. ------, "Most Wanted--Traffic Management's Magnificent 10," *Traffic Technology International*, February/March 2007, 31-35.

57. K. J. Button and D. A. Hensher, ed., *Handbook of Transport Systems and Traffic Control* (New York: Pergamon, 2001).

58. "Transportation Planning," *Wikipedia*, http://en.wikipedia.org/wiki/Transportation planning.

59. In Baltimore, the document is referred to as the CLRP, or the Constrained Long Range Plan. The constraint is a reference to funding limitations.

60. Telematics is the integrated use of telecommunications and information technology in vehicles to support the driving and control of the vehicles. It includes global positioning systems, cruise control, collision avoidance, vision enhancement, and other electronics systems.

61. Unattributed quote from ThinkExist.com, modified to replace the singular him with the plural they, http://thinkexist.com/quotes/with/keyword/customer/.

62. "Medtronic Annual Report 2007," *Medtronic Inc.*, Minneapolis, MN, http://216.139.227.101/interactive/mdt2007/.

63. The sources of some quotes are not provided to ensure their anonymity.

64. "Medtronic Home Page," *Medtronic Inc.*, http://www.medtronic.com/your-health/index.htm.

65. Intentionally anonymous.

66. "Customer Service," *State of Rhode Island, Department of Transportation*, http://www.dot.state.ri.us/customerservice/index.asp.

67. Contacting the DC Government, http://dc.gov/contact/index.shtm.

68. GRU--Electric Reliability, https://www.gru.com/YourHome/ProductsServices/ElectricNaturalGas/electricreliability.jsp.

69. African Proverb Quotes, *ThinkExist.com*, http://thinkexist.com/quotations/future/.

70. "Engineering the Megacity," *IEEE Spectrum* 44, no. 6 (2007): 24.

71. Ken Blanchard, *Buzzle.com*, http://www.buzzle.com/articles/teamwork-quotes-and-sayings.html.

72. A description of the Operations Academy can be found at: http://www.operationsacademy.org.

73. "Civil Engineering," *Wikipedia*, http://en.wikipedia.org/wiki/Civil_engineering.

74. "Undergraduate Admissions," *Princeton University*, http://www.princeton.edu/admission/whatsdistinctive/experience/certificate_programs/.

75. "Comedy Zone, Science and Technology Quotes," The quote is from David Sarnoff's (founder of NBC and president of RCA) associates in response to his request for an assessment of the commercial potential of the radio, http://www.comedy-zone.net/quotes/Science_and_Technology/science.htm.

76. This feature is already available as part of the suite of services included in the General Motors OnStar system and other similar systems.

77. Vehicle Infrastructure Integration website, *Research and Innovative Technology Administration (RITA)*, 2008, http://www.vehicle-infrastructure.org/vii-overview/.

78. "VII Research Program," August 2008, http://www.vehicle-infrastructure.org/program-information/vii-research-program-overview.pdf.

79. Two examples of such programs are the federal government's Small Business Innovative Research (SBIR), and the State of Maryland's Maryland Industrial Partners (MIPS) programs.

80. Thomas Watson, Sr., President of IBM, ThinkExist.com, http://thinkexist.com/quotes/with/keyword/organization/4.html.

81. "Notice of Initiating Rule Making, Notice of Comment Period and Notice of Rule Making Session," *Maryland Public Service Commission*, Administrative Document RM 43, January 12, 2011.

82. Establishing some of these requirements for a transportation utility is difficult because items such as incident clearance depend on the actions of others such as police, fire, emergency medical services (EMS), and others. However, only some of the items in the service interruption category rely on the actions of others.

83. "Utilities Mostly Maintain Reliability, Service Quality," press release by the New York State Public Service Commission, Albany, NY, June 17, 2010.

84. The System Average Interruption Duration Index (SAIDI) is often used as an alternative to the CAIDI. The SAIDI provides a more macroscopic view of the system reliability while the CAIDI provides a look at the impact of service disruptions on individual customers.

85. Reid Ewing, "Transportation Utility Fees," *Government Finance Review*, June 1, 1994, http://www.allbusiness.com/finance-insurance/465585-1.html.

86. "Trip Generation 8th Edition," *Institute of Transportation Engineers*, 2008, ISBN-13:978-1-933452-43-2, ISBN-10: 1-933452-43-9. Item IR-016F.

87. Parsons, Brinckerhoff, Tarnoff, et al., "Institutional Changes to Support Improved Congestion Management--Report and Guide," Strategic Highway Research Program 2, Project L06, Transportation Research Board, May 2009.

88. "Outsourcing," *Wikipedia*, http://en.wikipedia.org/wiki/Outsourcing.

89. "Plan Seeks to Employ More D.C. Residents--Council Chief Proposes New Residency Rules for City Contractors," *Washington Post*, January 19, 2011, B1.

90. Bach, Richard, *Wisdom Quotes*, http://www.wisdomquotes.com/topics/changegrowth/index3.html.

91. The David R. Goode National Transportation Policy Conference, *Miller Center of Public Affairs*, University of Virginia, September 10, 2009, http://millercenter.org/policy/transportation.

92. National Surface Transportation Policy and Revenue Study Commission, http://transportationfortomorrow.com/about/index.htm.

93. Commission Report, vol.1, 8, http://transportationfortomorrow.com/final_report/pdf/volume_1.pdf.

94. Brian Vastag, "Obama's Call for Innovation Follow Slump in Most Sectors," *The Washington Post*, January 28, 2011, A4.

95. "Annual Report on Initiatives for Outsourcing, Privatization and Downsizing within VDOT," HB 676 (2006), Report to the General Assembly of Virginia, November 2006, http://www.virginiadot.org/projects/resources/Outsourcing_Final_Report_-_VDOT_website.pdf.

96. "Transportation Partnership Opportunity Fund--Guidelines and Criteria," *The Commonwealth of Virginia*, September 2005, http://www.virginiadot.org/projects/resources/tpofImplementationGuidelines10-2005.pdf.

97. "Public-Private Partnerships," Innovative Project Delivery, *Federal Highway Administration*, http://www.fhwa.dot.gov/ipd/p3/index.htm.

CPSIA information can be obtained at www.ICGtesting.com
Printed in the USA
LVOW08*1828270913

354478LV00008B/276/P